# What Clients Say About Working With Jack…

"Anyone who is honest, willing to work hard and take suggestions could benefit from the coaching Jack provides. I recommend his services highly."

—Tyler G.
Owner, Pest Management Company

"Simply put if Jack can help me go from an average of 5-10% growth to 35% growth in each of the last two years during a recession he can help anybody. Jack knows the keys to helping small business people like me succeed. I would recommend Jack to any business person serious about going from where they are to where they want and can be."

– Ron F.
Owner, Telecom Services

"My business has grown 300% since I began meeting with Jack less than 3 months ago. He keeps me focused and on-track with what's important in my business."

– Dave B.
Independent Insurance Broker

"Sometimes you need someone who is willing to listen and provide focus. Someone who gets YOU and is willing to provide direction and solutions that work for you and not against you. The first full month of working with Jack my sales grew 150%, enough said."

– Greg S.
Insurance Agent

# Secrets of
# a Strategic
# Business Coach

## 10 Strategies to
## Build Your Business
## — *Faster!*

———— 𝒯 ————

Jack Rand
Strategic Business Coach

# COPYRIGHT AND DISCLAIMER

**Published by:**
Mo Betta Press, LLC
PO Box 16371
Colorado Springs, CO 80935-6371

Website: www.JackRand.com

## DISCLAIMER AND/OR LEGAL NOTICES:

# ACKNOWLEDGMENTS

*No one does this alone – no one.*

I am responsible for the content of this book. I could not have done it without all my clients who by just being themselves contributed to the development and content of my programs, coaching, and this work. You have taught me so much about determination and perseverance.

First, thanks to my wife, Marsha, for her patience and dedication. She spent way too many hours by herself while I wrote and then rewrote the manuscript after her thoughtful edits.

My friend, Gairy Gordon, who graciously allowed me to tell the Pikes Peak story my way.

To Doug Owens, who proves that a rocket scientist can learn to be a teddy bear, lead, and sell. Greg Smith, who started as a client and is now one of my best friends—the cabin is a blessing in many ways.

Grand Master Chae Hook Sung, who continues to teach me that there is always another ladder to climb.

Susan Hindman word smith, third set of eyes and comma specialist who helped make this a more readable work.

To Jeannie Long, who reminds me to never quit on your dreams.

# CONTENTS

# INTRODUCTION

What I'm about to share with you is the same process I use with my private clients to dramatically improve their overall results in life and business. These 10 Strategies are based on over 30 years of consulting, coaching, and personal sales production in a wide variety of businesses and industries, including being an MVP and Tops in Sales at Hewlett-Packard with a multimillion-dollar annual quota, a Sales Excellence Coach at HP, and a director of Sales and Marketing for a nationwide distributor.

One client tripled their sales, from $1 million to $3 million, in just 2 years; an attorney went from $0 to $15,000 per month in just 4 months; others now have the business and life of their dreams.

These 10 Strategies are designed to be used in concert with one another to help anyone achieve what they really want. You may be a new or seasoned sales professional, a new or serial entrepreneur, a team builder or sales manager, or a network marketer. It also doesn't matter what your age or physical ability: Don't let excuses hold you back—again.

These strategies can work for you, and the best time to start applying them is now. If you don't, you'll be having the same conversation with yourself again next year.

To Your Success,

*Jack*

Jack Rand
Strategic Business Coach

# 1

# Know What You Want

―― 𝒯 ――

*"If we are facing the right direction all we have
to do is keep on walking."*
– Zen Proverb

In January 2010 I had an epiphany. I had just finished putting together my first **Personal Results System™** and was writing the instructions so my clients would have written directions on how to use it.

In a flash of insight, it came to me: *Most people think of results and accomplishment as straight line.* For example, 500 to 1,000 on a graph can be a straight line. In reality, though, it's a cycle with seven distinct steps.

As I worked through the process, the *seven steps* became the *7-Step Personal Results Cycle™* I now use with clients to build their **Personal Results System** as a strategy to transform their effectiveness, their productivity, and their life to have the results they really want.

The **Personal Results System** is a mindful intentional strategy to optimize your life and outcomes. Mindful means to be awake, aware. Intentional means consciously, purposefully.

Optimize means to make as effective, perfect, or useful as possible, to make the best of.

Let's take a look at the *7-Step Personal Results Cycle.*

**Step 1: Vision**

## Vision

*Personal Results Cycle*™

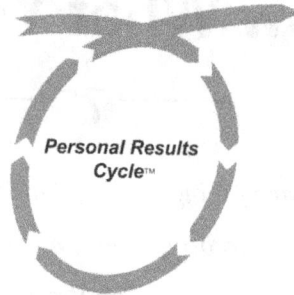

*Vision is not seeing things as they are, but as they will be.*

**Vision:** the act or power of anticipating that which will or may come to be

Your *Vision* is how you see your future in your mind. Usually, you see and feel yourself in the life-style you want to have, doing the things you want to do, and with whom you want to do them. Believe it or not, your *Vision* most often determines the direction you take and the *Results* you achieve.

Elite athletes and high-performance teams such as the US Air Force Thunderbirds Flight Demonstration Team use visualization techniques to improve their performance. Before each show the Thunderbird pilots sit around a table as their commander/leader takes them through an eyes-closed rehearsal of their flight. The result is consistent excellence show after show.

Another example is Olympic skier Lindsey Vonn. You can often see her close her eyes and use her hands to weave down the slope's twists, turns, and bumps to the finish line. She's rehearsing in her mind. Her body then knows what to do far more automatically and faster than conscious thought can guide her. This process has helped her to win Olympic medals and championships.

Your *vision* for life and business is critical to your success. The more vividly you can see it in your mind's eye, the more real and achievable it becomes.

**Step 2: Purpose**

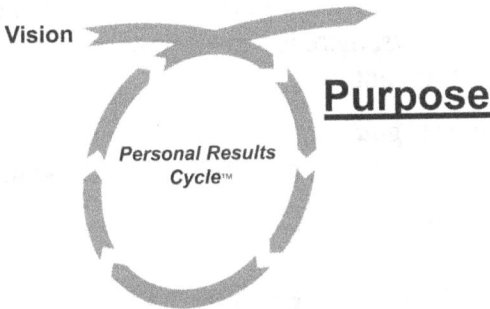

Vision

**Purpose**

*Personal Results Cycle*™

*Using your heart is more powerful than using your head.*

***Purpose*:** a heartfelt statement of your intention and direction

Your *purpose* comes from your heart and answers the question, why you want to achieve your *goals* and *vision*. *Purpose* is so powerful that every Special Forces unit worldwide has their own way of testing for its members' resolve.

One of the most notorious is the US Navy SEALs Hell Week. It starts on a Sunday night and lasts until the following Friday afternoon. During the week, trainees only get 4 total hours of sleep, and they fight exhaustion, delirium, and hypothermia. They're constantly on the move, they're in and out of the ocean, and all the while, they're harassed to quit by the instructors. During this process, an individual's deep desire to serve and their tenacity are dramatically tested.

A class starting with 120-130 qualified candidates will have only 20-30 remaining at the end of the week. The men with the deepest desire make it through what may be the toughest week in the world.

When the going gets tough, and it will, you're more likely to achieve your objective when your intention and desire are strong enough. While there's no guarantee that with such a strong resolve you'll reach your *goals*, there is a great possibility you'll quit before you reach them if it's not.

When you set *goals* from your heart that fulfill your *purpose*, the odds are much greater that you will achieve them.

### Step 3: Goals

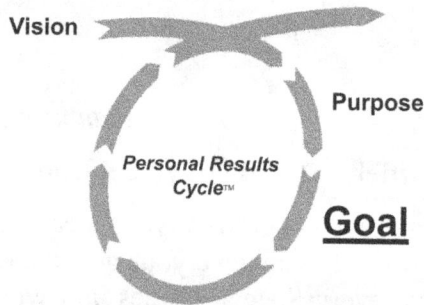

Vision    Purpose

*Personal Results Cycle*™

**Goal**

*Once your purpose is strong enough you will set a goal.*

**Goal**: a specific objective or target that drives action

One of the first conversations I have with clients is about their *goals*. The reason I do this is because *goals* are one of the primary motivators of action.

Let me explain. Suppose you're out driving around and it's now 11:30 a.m. and you're hungry. What becomes your goal? Get something to eat—NOW!

You realize that you have some choice in the matter and start reviewing your options: Option 1—eat the protein bar in your bag; Option 2—go to the convenience store and buy a bar or a bag of chips or one of those sandwiches in the display case; Option 3—go to the nearest fast-food place and, again, eat a meal that may or may not work for your diet; Option 4—go to your favorite restaurant, which may take 45 minutes or so and cost more or... You get the point. Your goal, "get something to eat now," is driving your action.

Every day you are setting small *goals* and automatically begin to find ways to achieve them, and, in this case, you get something to eat.

Other examples in your daily life include:

Get to work on time.

Make dinner for the kids.

Complete the project by Friday.

Design a new web page.

Complete 5 phone calls.

**Why Is It So Difficult to Reach Other Bigger Goals?**

The most common reason you struggle too much trying to reach bigger *goals* is because the goal is too big and you don't have a realistic Action Plan to achieve it.

As an illustration: Imagine a horizontal bar 12 feet from the floor that looks like the high horizontal high bar you would see in Olympic gymnastics. Could you jump up and grab it right now? Probably not. (The NBA basketball rim is 10 feet from the floor.)

However, if you built a set of stairs with achievable steps, you could climb right up and grab the bar easily.

### Goals Provide Structure

To see structure at work, look at how you would behave if you said, "I must go to the grocery market sometime." Would it be different than if you said, "I must go to the grocery market by 5 p.m. today?"

The odds are your behavior would be markedly different to get to the grocery market by 5 p.m. today. It would be more urgent and focused than having to go "sometime."

### Goals Formula

Clear, sharp, achievable *goals* provide the structure to drive action and are the key to being more effective.

The basic *Goals* formula is expressed simply as:

Item X by Time Y

This means you want Item X by Time Y.

For example; you want an Item X (New Client) by Time Y (Noon Friday).

This statement is a clear set of instruction to execute, and the odds of achieving your goal are dramatically improved.

If you have the goal of "increasing your sales," then anything will do, even just 1 dollar. On the other hand, if want to increase your sales by $10,000 per month by 31 July of this year at noon, the odds of you actually achieving your goal is much greater.

**Step 4: Action**

Vision

Purpose

*Personal Results Cycle*™

Goal

## Action

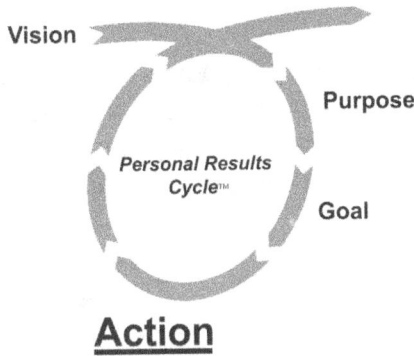

*Once you have set a goal, you will naturally take action.*

*Action*: energetic performing or taking part

**Three types of *Actions* are required to reach your goals.**

- Physical
- Mental
- Speech

All three must be in alignment to be effective.

*Physical* action means you are doing the right activities and tasks to achieve your goals. This includes, and is not limited to, attending meetings, meeting people, writing letters and marketing material, sending promotional announcements and marketing materials, closing sales, etc. You get the idea.

*Mental* activity means to use the right intention, focus, and desire to achieve your goals.

*Speech* means to use the right voice both in oral and written forms to promote your cause. It can be at an event where you're the speaker, it could be meeting people to enroll them in your program, or the written message you send in thank-you notes, promotional materials, etc.

Here's the BIG POINT: When all the things you do are in alignment with each other and done in sufficient quantity and quality, the odds of getting the results you want go way up. If they're not in alignment, it takes longer and the odds go down that you'll achieve your goals on time.

### Step 5: Result

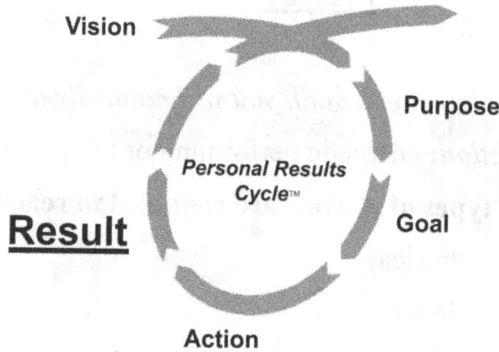

*For every Action, there is an opposite and equal reaction or Result.*

**Result**: a consequence of actions, outcome

From Newton's third law of motion we know that, for every action, there is an equal and opposite reaction. In this sense, the fifth step of the *7-Step Personal Results Cycle* means that your *Results* are a consequence of your *Actions*.

During the coaching process, I spend time with clients discussing their *Goals*, their *Actions*, and the *Results* they're getting to find out what's working and what's not.

For example, if your goal is 5 and you got 10, we know that something you're doing is working real well and let's do more of that. On the other hand, if you wanted 5 and got 1, then we have to figure out what didn't work and fix it.

### What's Working and What's Not

To sort out what's working and what's not, we must see in detail the actions you're taking and the results they're producing. We use a *13-Week Dashboard* to do this, and you can get one at www.JackRand.com/Tools/. By tracking your activities and results, we can quickly sort out the most effective ones and eliminate what doesn't serve you.

Working with a pest control company one of the owners was responsible for sales. They wanted to grow the company by focusing on attaining new commercial contracts that required monthly service. As he began tracking his prospecting activity week to week, he noticed that he was off track more than on track with his business calls. He noticed that they had some strong months and some weak ones. As we did the research, he discovered that the weak or slow sales months were followed by low sales call numbers.

To fix the problem, he now calls on a consistent number of new clients each week and month to provide consistent new client acquisition. As a result, the monthly revenue has grown over 10 times in one year.

### Adjust as Required

Suppose it's noon and you have a 2 p.m. appointment in a city 60 miles away. You're traveling by car, so obviously you know it's going to take an hour to get there at 60 miles an hour. During the trip, you notice that your speed is only 45 miles an hour and you stopped for lunch along the way.

You're somewhere in between where you were and where you're going. What do you need to do to get to your appointment on time?

A. Knowing where you are.

B. Knowing the distance to the location.

With these two pieces of information, it's rather easy to determine how fast you must travel to get there on time.

What's the point, you ask? The point here is that to achieve your goals, you must know how fast you're traveling to achieve your goals on time. And most of you don't know how fast you're going, so it's impossible to get there on time.

This approach is used by sports teams who constantly adjust to changing game conditions, racing teams that adjust to problems and race conditions, and airline pilots who adjust their course and speed.

For example, if you are flying from Denver to Hawaii, your plane is on course about 1 percent of the time. The plane is constantly moving left and right of its compass heading and up and down due to wind currents. If the course is off by only 1 degree and not adjusted, you will miss the Hawaiian Islands by 120 miles. And that, my friend, will be a very different vacation than the one you planned.

### Step 6: Complete and Celebrate

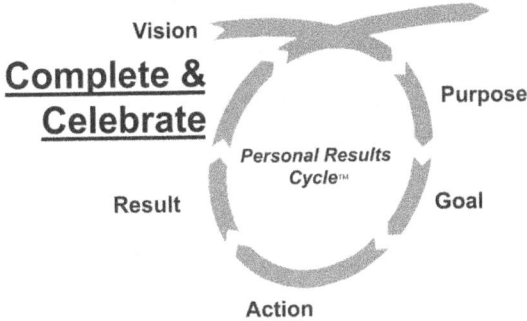

Personal Results Cycle™ diagram: Vision, Purpose, Goal, Action, Result, with "Complete & Celebrate" highlighted.

*Give yourself a spiritual pat on the back.*

**Complete:** to declare tasks, activities, and *goals*, done or finished

**Celebrate:** to praise widely, laud, glorify, honor, applaud, commend

We've all been children, and many of you have children. When kids are about 2 years old, we teach them to brush their teeth and they pretty much make a mess of it. We love them, so we clean them up and say "Good job" and send them on their way.

Why do we do say "Good job" when we know they made a mess?

We also know that the tooth brushing probably wasn't perfect.

Why do we say "Good job" every time?

The answer is that we want to praise them so they feel good about the job and come back again willingly.

Yet, what do we say to ourselves, as adults, when we finish a job?

Usually it's something like:

"OK, what's next?"

"That was a mess…"

"I wish I did that faster…"

"Yikes, I'm late for my appointment!"

The list goes on and on and on. So, why do we treat ourselves that way? It seems like such drudgery!

Well, somewhere along the way, we adopted this self-talk behavior. I argue it doesn't serve us, and in fact it's not useful for being happy and fulfilled with your work and life.

## Your Foundation Is Built in Layers

The way you treat and talk to yourself forms the foundation of your self-esteem. Each time you say to yourself, in some way, that you're not good enough, you become "NOT GOOD ENOUGH."

These words and phrases may be only be as thin as a sheet of paper and by themselves easily torn to shreds, but layer upon layer they become as difficult to tear as a thick book. These judgments are toxic and keep you stuck.

## The Good News

So, here's an alternative behavior to be more productive, be happy, and have more fun. Every time you finish a task or activity say, *"Yippee"* in your head. Yep, a little *"Yippee" Dance* in your head, and sometimes say it out loud. Try it right now. How did it feel?

Now imagine if you said *"Yippee!"* every time you finished something. Something as mundane as doing the dishes, making that phone call, or brushing your teeth. Do you think you're going to feel better about yourself? Will your confidence grow? I think so.

## The Beginning of Your New Foundation

Give yourself a virtual pat on the back to honor your progress with a *"Yippee" Dance.* Every time you complete a phone call, say *"Yippee"* to yourself.

Every time you complete an activity or task, say a *"Yippee"* to yourself. For example, you go to a networking meeting and meet someone new. Give yourself a *"Yippee!"*

When you do this for just one day, just one week, how do you think you're going to feel?

Yep, you'll be invigorated, excited, and ready to take on more. It never fails. You don't have to wait for someone else to acknowledge you—do it yourself! When clients execute this prescription, they immediately begin doing better at work, at home, and at play.

### *"Yippee!"*

I give the *"Yippee"* assignment to my clients, during my workshops and speaking engagements. When I check in to see how it works, everyone says that it really works while they shake their head up and down with a big smile.

If you get nothing else out of this book or system, try the *"Yippee"* for one week. Experience how it feels for yourself. Then send me an email to Support@JackRand.com and let me know how it works for you. Start now… You just finished this step, so give yourself a *"Yippee"* as a secret salute to yourself.

## Step 7: Renewal and Gratitude

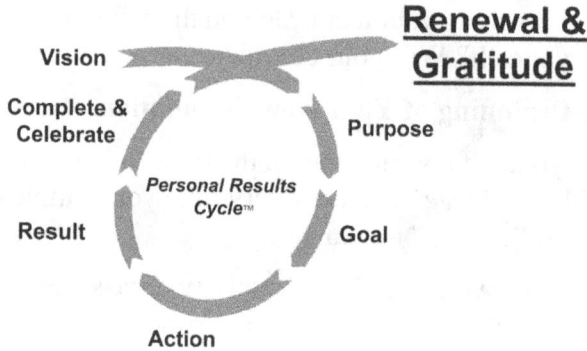

*Take care of yourself to consistently achieve at the highest levels.*

**Renewal:** to restore or replenish; to bring back to an original condition of freshness and vigor

**Gratitude:** a feeling of gratefulness or thankfulness, for gifts or favors

Suppose you had the newest high-tech flashlight available. It's smaller, weighs less, is 4 times brighter, and lasts 7 times longer than the nearest competitor. Pretty cool, huh!

What happens if you leave your badass flashlight on all the time?

It runs out of power and won't work until you recharge or change the battery.

On the face of it, this is a simple example. If we compare the battery to ourselves, something else becomes evident. We don't treat ourselves the same way! We push and push and push, then wonder why we're so exhausted.

When my clients tell me they're tired all the time, I ask them a simple question: "What are you doing to renew yourself?"

The answer is usually a blank stare and a mumbled question asking, "What do you mean?"

I answer, "What are you doing to take care of yourself? How much time on a weekly basis do you take, just for you, to do something you love and have fun doing?"

The answer: a weak "Not much."

When I ask them to take two hours per week for themselves, just two hours, their productivity improves and we didn't change anything mechanical.

Here's why. When I was in my first year of college, I was installing a clutch on my car. There was a bolt for a bracket that looked easy to put in, but try after try I couldn't get it to go. I'd been working on it most of the day. I was tired, frustrated, and my fingers were not working very well. So, about 7 p.m. I quit for the day and cleaned up.

The next day, I decided to give the stubborn bolt one quick try before I left for school. In seconds, the bolt was in place! With a big smile, I zoomed off to class.

Have you ever been in a similar place? You must read a book or document, and the words gray out or turn into Chinese characters, and you don't read Chinese. You try several times, squint your eyes, and still no help. So you give up for the night. The next morning, you look at the document and you breeze through it in minutes.

### Renewal Is a Declaration

When my son was young, I read to him before bed. His favorite story was "Postman Pig." It's about a cute little pig that delivers mail to the shops and stores in his little town. Jonathan, of course, would seem to be sleeping, and then I would make

15

something up in the simple story. All of a sudden, he was wide awake telling me that the alligator did not eat the pig, it wasn't in the story, and to read it right. OK, I got busted on that one.

I noticed that when I was reading to him, if I held it in my mind as a "to do," it became a chore. On the other hand, when I declared it "fun time," I had a lot more fun with it. I think he did too.

The point here is that renewal is a declaration. You can declare something as renewal and have more fun doing it—even raking the leaves. When you're in-the-moment raking the leaves, you'll notice more about the trees, the grass, or lack thereof, and you may remember fond times when you played in the leaf piles in autumn when you were a kid.

You can also just do something fun. Recently I had a meeting cancel at the last minute. So, I went to the office supply store to buy some colored paper. On my way to the car, I noticed a hobby shop next door and stopped in. I looked at remote control helicopters. Big ones and small ones. I checked the prices and talked with the sales clerk.

I left 30 minutes later, thrilled. I didn't buy one that day, but it was so different from my usual routine. It was fun and unexpected. I felt renewed.

**Recharge Your Energy**

Renewal is honoring your mind, body, and spirit by doing something fun, unexpected, outside your normal routine. For some, it's taking a hot bath with candles and a glass of wine—luxurious! For you, it may be taking a drive in your prized hot rod or flying a remote control model airplane. Start today by asking yourself:

What can I do for a little getaway?

What would be fun?

I found this when the movie *Star Wars* first came out. I was selling commercial real estate, and spontaneously took Wednesday afternoon off and went to the movies by myself. I had the best time sitting in the center of the near empty theater, eating a big box of buttered popcorn with a big soda watching Hans Solo and R2D2. I felt refreshed, energized, and eager to get back to work.

Today I'll grab my wife, and we'll take Wednesdays off and go to the movies. It's great fun. Oh, I usually don't know what's playing, so we just pick something we think is good. It's surprisingly fun!

### Sustaining Momentum

You may believe that taking time off will ruin your momentum, stall your flow. What I've found with myself and clients is that the break you take actually restores energy and provides a fresh perspective.

When you don't take a break is when you start spending too much time on things that could be done faster when you're fresh. The US Navy SEALs have a saying, "Tired men make mistakes." That's one of the reasons they are known for their fitness by Special Forces units around the world.

The real key to being consistently productive and to sustaining the momentum you're building each day, week, and month is to take care of yourself. Support your mind, body, and spirit so you can perform at your highest level possible.

### Diet

Eating right is a form of renewal. The real trick is to find a diet and eating schedule that works for you to maintain your energy and health. Everyone and everyone's body is different, so finding the right combination of foods and times to eat are essential. If you don't, you could find yourself running out of energy at three in the afternoon and wonder why. The answer may be that you did not eat lunch or what you had for lunch.

WARNING: If you don't take the time to eat properly, your body and health will suffer. Don't wait until your body tells you by sickness, disease, or sleepiness.

### Gratitude

Research has shown that feeling thankful for what you have and the gifts you have been given opens you up spiritually to receive more good things.

Feeling grateful also wards off feelings of depression for those who are altruistic. Being altruistic in this sense means to be working from your *purpose* and providing value, sometimes without much in return initially.

Taking time each day to express being thankful is an effective way to build the habit and become more aware of how grateful you are.

Some experts recommend keeping a gratitude journal and writing something that you're feeling thankful for, no matter how small, each day. They don't have to be big things; they can be small and meaningful actions, words, praise, or items—they add up over time, and you're much further ahead than doing nothing.

Every night I silently ask, "What am I thankful for today?" Whatever comes up in my mind is *what* I go with. I'm often surprised at the answers and rest more comfortably when I'm feeling grateful instead of stressed.

I find that I'm more tolerant, more giving, and more appreciative. And it's easier to give my love and time to those who need it. It's especially powerful when I'm not expecting anything in return—it's a gift from me.

## Tithing

In a general sense, tithing means to give a part of something freely, a contribution. It's a gift from you to others to help them grow. It can be money, time, or things. It can be to an organization or individuals.

Originally, the tithing amount was a percentage of your crops or cattle to the church. Now it can be 10 percent of your income. However, the big point is to give what you can and feel comfortable doing it in an ongoing way to the charity or organization of your choice, and feel blessed to do so.

Several years ago, we donated each month to a nonprofit fund and were privileged to support a young Indian girl through grade and middle school. She often would send us a picture of herself and her family, and tell us of the gifts she had purchased for her family as well. While we never met her, she was part of our family and we're honored to have helped her.

## Pay It Forward

Pay it forward is a way of giving to another in advance of a request, without expecting something in return. Pay it forward can be expressed as buying a stranger coffee, a meal, or something they need and cannot afford right now that will further their growth.

Recently I went to one of my local coffee shops to meet a client. While standing online, I noticed a sign that requested a donation of a cup of coffee for someone who needed it and didn't have the money to pay for it. So, I put an extra cup on my bill. I don't know who got the coffee. I don't even know when it happened. I do know that I still feel grateful to be able to help another.

## Lend It Forward

The lend it forward concept is not new. Benjamin Franklin is reported to have used the same system. Here's how it works.

When you lend money to another, instead of having it paid back to you, have the other party lend it to another in need. This concept has the possibility of creating an eternal monetary support system.

Being generous with your time, money, and possessions is a powerful and meaningful way to contribute to others and feel grateful.

### Thanksgiving

Have you ever taken the time to serve Thanksgiving dinner at your local rescue mission? I can tell you firsthand that this is a way to genuinely feel thankful and appreciate all that you have.

Here in Colorado, the winters can get very cold. In January, for example, the nighttime temperature can be 20°F below zero several days in a row. When I'm serving, I see firsthand how people are struggling without hot food and jackets to keep them warm in the cold winter. I'm thankful for what I have and can give. It certainly puts whatever challenge I have going on at the time in perspective.

### *Go Have Fun*

We all have stuff we have to do, no matter how much we love our work, and we have deadlines. Americans seem to live to work, and they can't seem to figure out why they're so tired all the time.

Ask yourself, "Are you living to work or working to live?"

If you're living to work, perhaps it's time to have some fun. Life is too short to be so burdened all the time. Maybe you can't chuck the job or change the business overnight, but you can carve out some time to do some things you love and have fun doing.

I hereby give you permission to *Go Have Fun.*

## Continuous Improvement

The core philosophy threaded through the *7-Step Personal Results Cycle* is *kaizen,* a Japanese word that means continuous improvement. The *kaizen* includes learning from both your wins and your failures.

Mary, a financial advisor, was overall doing well with her performance, but she had a terrible habit of quitting on her goals if she thought that she would not achieve them by the third week of the month. Not just once—every month.

She wondered why consistently achieving her goals was so elusive. Once I spotted the pattern, I told her that she's killing her momentum when she quits on her goals. What she didn't see was that this month's activity sets up the sales for the next three months. So every time she stopped, she killed her progress for the next three months.

We reviewed her goals to be sure they were the right size, and the next month she fixed the habit and went on to win a contest and a company paid vacation. What a great way to complete, celebrate, and renew.

I have not found that it does any good whatsoever to beat yourself up about a failure. Notice professional athletes when they make a mistake or lose a game: They let it go and look for ways to improve for next time, and so should you.

When you're using goals as tools to live your vision, you're going to find out what's working and what's not working. These are not right-or-wrong judgments of what you have or have not done, or of how well you did or didn't do something. Judgments keep you trapped and stuck.

When you use the continuous improvement mind-set, each iteration becomes an opportunity to optimize your life, your productivity, and your business.

# The *7-Step Personal Results Cycle*

## Optimize Your Potential

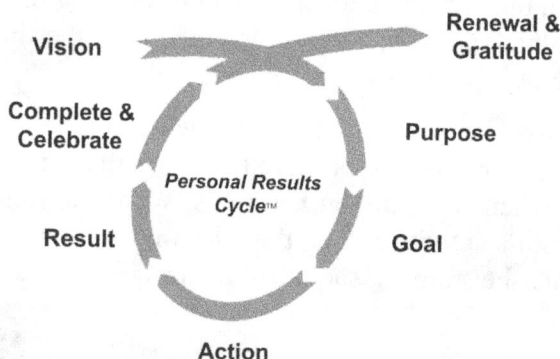

## Continuous Improvement

### Transform your life and outcomes

1. *Know* what you want.

2. *Know* why you want it.

3. *Set Goals* to achieve your *vision*.

4. *Take the right Action* to achieve your *Goals*.

5. *Track your Results.*

6. *Complete and Celebrate* your progress.

7. *Renew yourself and be Grateful* for what you have.

Leverage both wins and failures to optimize your results.

# 2

# Fight for Your Goals

———— 𝒯 ————

*"The meaning of life is to find your gift.*
*The purpose of life is to give it away."*
– Pablo Picasso

At my core, I'm a teacher. My purpose is to deliver what I've learned in a way that others can use it to fulfill their purpose.

I've set many goals, achieved many goals, and missed many goals. What I've learned is that missing a goal is not the end of the world—goals are simply tools used to drive action.

Some of you quit on your goals because you become disappointed, frustrated, and even angry when you don't accomplish them. Goals are a way of knowing how strong you are.

A few years ago, I wanted to climb Pikes Peak. I had already attempted it twice before and quit both times because I just was not in good enough physical shape to complete the ascent.

I was determined. So, I went to the gym and talked with a trainer. We worked out a plan to build my strength and endurance so I could summit the elusive peak.

As I was working out with the weights, I realized that I couldn't complete the sets as I thought they should be completed. Frustrated, I gathered up my courage to talk with my trainer. I told him about my failures at working with the weights. What he told me was shocking.

"You're supposed to fail," he said.

"What? Supposed to fail?!" I said.

"Yes," he explained.

Then he said, "When you're training with weights, you're working your muscles until they fail at each set and weight. For example, if you're doing three sets of 12 reps, when the weight is right you can expect to do 12 reps the first set, 10 the second set, and maybe 8 the third set.

"When you work your muscles until they fail, or you can't do any more, your muscles will respond by getting stronger. Over time you will gain strength and endurance. But you must take time off to let the muscles rest and grow. Too much of a good thing and the process breaks down the muscle, it takes longer to recover, and you're prone to injury."

I think my head started to jerk like a robot with a programing error. I'd been thinking about this all wrong: Instead of trying to avoid failure, I should seek it out—and I can be really successful by going for failure.

I must say that this bit of reprograming stretched my thinking again. I was excited to go to the gym and learn where I fail and was actually proud of myself when my muscles stopped working.

As I progressed, my strength increased. On exercises that I used to do 15-pound reps, I was now doing 20 pounds. I used to envy the guys that were doing that much weight, and now I was doing it too. Yea, at last I was doing big boy weights.

Another part of my plan was cardio workouts. My trainer said I needed to be at 12 degrees of incline for 30 minutes to make it to the top. Well, being a bit of an overachiever now and looking for failure, I worked into 45 minutes at 15 degrees. I did not want to fail on the mountain—the big goal.

I must admit that 15 degrees did not come easy. I increased my incline only when my heart rate monitor said it was OK. I did not want to kill myself before the event.

I also had extra help. My good friend, Gairy, and I would hike the Incline, an abandoned railroad in Manitou Springs, Colorado, that provides an incredibly intense workout, to get into climbing shape.

The Incline starts at 6,600 feet and climbs just over 2,000 feet in 3/4 of a mile. There is a bailout point about 2/3 of the way up that connects with Barr Trail and is the way down. Gairy, who was extremely fit, could climb the Incline easily, while I would have to bail out about 2/3 of the way up on my first attempts.

Great news! I completed the Incline before my Pikes Peak summit attempt and deemed myself ready for the assault.

About 5 a.m. on a chilly Saturday morning in July, I was at the Barr Trail trailhead in Manitou Springs, to begin the climb up Pikes Peak. Gairy was parking the car, so I started out alone. He promised to catch up quickly.

The trail rises 7,800 vertical feet over its 12.5 miles to the summit of Pikes Peak at 14,115 feet. This is one of the most challenging 14'ers in Colorado because of the trail length and elevation gain.

Gairy caught up with me in about an hour. At 8:50 a.m., we arrived at Barr Camp, having climbed 3,800 vertical feet over 6.5

miles. The elevation was now 10,200 feet and the air thinner than when we began. The summit was still 6 miles away.

We took the opportunity to eat, rest, and hydrate before we continued on to our next goal called the A Frame, at the edge of tree line. The next 3 miles took us 40 minutes. The elevation was now 11,500 feet, the air was thinner, and I noticed how much harder it was to hike than before. We again rested, ate, and hydrated to prepare us to achieve the next goal on our quest.

The temperature had dropped 20 degrees, and I put on my fleece vest to keep warm. To be safe, we had to summit by 2 p.m. to avoid the afternoon thunderstorms that move in almost every day with lightning that can strike exposed hikers.

The final challenge before the summit is the 16 Golden Stairs. The stairs refer to a set of switchbacks that take you to the peak. This is the most difficult section of the trail and may hold snow even in late July.

We started our ascent on the one-mile set of stairs at 13,300 feet elevation. Just 815 vertical feet more to the summit. This was by far the most difficult physical challenge I have attempted.

I did summit the 14,153-foot Mt. Belford a few years earlier, and it wasn't this tough. I did paddle on an outrigger canoe team in Southern California two summers in a row. Our longest race of the season was from Long Beach, California, to Catalina Island, a distance of about 31 miles, and that was not this tough.

As we tackled the switchbacks, I was really tired. I thought of quitting and realized that I'd have to hike all the way back down the trail. I had done that twice before and remembered how much my knees hurt. I remembered how I felt when I had quit before. Now I was so close, just one more switchback. Then as I rested, I realized there were several more to go.

No matter how hard it was, I kept on going. When I would stop to rest, Gairy was always with me asking, "How are you doing?" My reply was always "I'm good," no matter how I felt.

You must understand that Gairy is from Jamaica. Why he was climbing this mountain with me is still a mystery. Maybe it's like the Jamaican bobsled team, or maybe it's because he's my friend.

Turn after turn, I kept going. Then at the last turn, I saw another friend from work encouraging me to keep going by telling me that I could make it. He said he would give me a cheer when I arrived. He kept it up until I met him at the summit. His cheer: a quiet "Yippee." "That's it?" I said. "Yep," he replied. He smiled and turned his attention to the next climber. I saluted him in good cheer as Gairy and I slowly walked to the summit store to look for some doughnuts.

It was now 1:21 p.m. I had met my big goal of summiting before 2 p.m. I called my wife to tell her the news and that I was safe. I also told her this was my hardest physical challenge so far and got emotional. Gairy was with me smiling his *be happy* grin.

Gairy and I rode in a van down the mountain on the same steep, twisting road—with no safety barriers—used for the annual Pikes Peak Hill Climb. As we slowly made our way, I began to grasp just how far we had come.

Today, as I drive around Colorado Springs, I can see Pikes Peak. It's big. Sometimes I remember that I climbed the monster and marvel at how tall it is, as I say to myself, "I climbed that," with a sense of confidence and joy and a result that I own that didn't come easy.

## Climb Your Mountain One Step at a Time

When I climbed Pikes Peak, I had a clear goal: Summit Pikes Peak by 2 p.m. or sooner that day. It fulfilled the basic goal formula: Item X by Time Y. Item "Summit Pikes Peak" by Time "2 p.m. or sooner."

I prepared physically by working out at the gym and I had a series of interim objectives or steps to achieve along the way. The first was Barr Camp, then the A Frame, then the 16 Golden Stairs. Each one moved me closer toward my final objective, the summit.

Climbing a mountain may not ever be one of your goals. However, the philosophy, process, and reasoning remain the same for any goal you set and sincerely want to achieve.

## The Gap

The *Gap* is the distance from where you are right now to where you want to go. To close your *gap,* build your success in steps or stages that you can achieve and that leverage on one another. For example, when working with a financial advisor, their goals are set up so that each quarter is a little bolder than the previous one. When added up, their run-rate is on track to reach their 12-Month Goals.

## Use an *Action Plan*

The major problem I see with having big goals is that you usually don't have an *Action Plan* to achieve them. An *Action Plan* lays out what you're going to do by when to reach your goals. It's your road map for achievement.

I argue that you would not be going on a camping trip without some planning and a map, so why not plan your success?

And put it all in one place instead of on scraps of paper and sticky notes to yourself that are scattered about.

## *Action Plan* Key Components

*Start/End Dates:* Time frame start to finish

*Name and Organization:* Who's accountable

*Purpose:* A heartfelt statement of intention and direction

*Goals:* What you want to achieve by when

*Activities:* Exactly what you're going to do to achieve your goals

*Results:* What you actually achieved compared to your goals

*Projects:* Anything that takes more than one activity to complete and is working ON your business

*Adjustments & Lessons:* What you're going to change to reach your goal when you're off track

*Gratitude:* Giving appreciation for this opportunity

### Put a Stake in the Ground

An *Action Plan* becomes a blueprint to build your dream. If you have ever seen a highway being built, you'll first see a series of wooden stakes pounded into the ground that lay out the direction and grade of the roadway. The road graders follow the stakes to create the roadbed.

Early explorers would put a flag on the land they were claiming for their country. So, creating and using an *Action Plan* is a symbolic way of putting a stake in the ground to "Claim Your Dream."

### Goals Are Tools That Drive Action

Some of you may see goals as winning or losing. If you achieve your goal you win, and if you don't you lose. This is quite simple on the face of it. However, seeing goals this way distracts you from how powerful and useful goals can be to fulfill your vision.

When you see goals as tools to drive action, you can then use goals to leverage your productivity. For example, you have set a goal of 5 new customers and $5,000 in new sales by Friday at noon (Item X by Time Y). With your best effort, you only get 3 new customers and $3,000 in new sales. In the win/lose model, you lose. In the *tools* model, you win.

You win because the truth is that you are now three closer to your overall goal than you were before. And you have the opportunity to see what's working and what's not, so you can improve your performance for next time.

In sports, the coach will usually say to the team at the end of the game, whether they won or lost, that there is more work to do to get better. She'll say we'll review the video of the game and figure out how to improve for the next game.

Time after time, as the coaches and the team review their progress and make corrections, the team does get better. The team's goal is to win the next game—sometimes they do, and sometimes they don't. They still keep improving.

# Continuous Improvement

After World War II, the Japanese economy was in ruins. With the help of the US and other world economic powers, the Japanese rebuilt their country into a world-class economic powerhouse.

*Kaizen* is the Japanese word for continuous improvement. It's a philosophy that leverages your success as well as your failures. During this process, most of you run into your most deeply held beliefs about achievement and success. One of the biggest ones is failure.

## Learning How to Use Failure

Failing is one of the ways we learn and, by itself, is not a bad thing. If we throw a ball and it's left of the target, the smart adjustment is to aim more to the right next time. If we overcook our breakfast, the next time we may use a lower heat or not cook it as long.

The trick is to learn from the failure—that's it. If you don't learn from your failures, then you are sure to repeat them. One of the definitions of insanity is to repeat the same actions and expect a different result.

I knew that if I really wanted to summit Pikes Peak, then I must improve my physical conditioning and change my mind-set about failure. I learned from each attempt. I didn't take it personally; it was part of the process. It took time and patience because I had to change my old perspective on failure every time I worked out.

If you're a personal producer such as a financial advisor or insurance agent, you can change failure into an opportunity to learn about yourself and your process. If you're a team manager, you can use failure for you and your team to learn about what works and what doesn't work to improve your overall performance.

As you work on your projects and goals, look to see how you can improve your results on every cycle, and you'll be surprised at how far you can go in just 90 days.

What helps to keep you stuck is your fear of failing. To grow, you must experiment.

## Being Curious

Some say that curiosity killed the cat. Curiosity also invented the helicopter, developed a cure for polio, and spurred the space program, which required the miniaturization of electronics that included transistors and the transistor radio, handheld computers, home computers, the Internet, and so on. If it wasn't for curiosity, we probably wouldn't have cell phones and flat screen TVs.

In my view, being curious is far more useful than dangerous. It's one of the ways we learn and is useful for finding ways out of your self-imposed box.

## The 80/30 Rule

Researchers found that if you make a public commitment to do something, 80 percent or more of the time you will achieve it. If you make a commitment and keep it to yourself, then 30 percent or less of the time you'll keep your pledge.

As an example, suppose you say to yourself that you're going to the gym on Tuesday at 8 a.m. to work out. How likely is it that you're going to show up at the gym? Now, if you talk with your friend and make a commitment to meet at the gym at 8 a.m. on Tuesday, how likely are you to be there?

The odds are 80 percent or greater that you will make it to the gym on time with your public commitment to your friend versus keeping it to yourself. Keeping quiet allows you a way out if you change your mind, don't feel like it, the weather is gloomy, or whatever you make up to not be there.

The key factor here is accountability. Accountability means going public with your goals to another person so they can hold you to your word and commitment. Kept secret, it's way too easy to quit, to stop when it gets tough, or to just not do it. Who's going to know if you quit?

As a professional coach, I work with clients every day on their goals and commitments. We use these opportunities to learn what's working for them and what's not. It's a time of challenge and fun. Their growth amazes and inspires me.

I have a friend who committed to raise money for cancer research. He sent emails and talked with people about his event. The last I heard, he surpassed his goal by double. If he had not gone public, he wouldn't have had the same response.

# Achievement Breakthrough

Researchers found that students who were acknowledged only for their grades on a test or project with praise such as "You're so smart" were more likely to quit when they ran into a tough problem or did not receive a good grade on a subsequent test or project.

However, the students who were acknowledged for their effort or work, such as "Good work on that," no matter what the grade or outcome, stayed with their projects longer even when they were more difficult or challenging. They also had better self-esteem.

Putting an extreme amount of attention and intention on getting the results you want can cause problems. If you don't achieve it, you may be disappointed, depressed, or even angry. Here's the good news: Focus on the work to do to achieve your goal to make more progress and avoid depression. The truth is that no matter what the outcome, you're now closer to your overall goal than before.

It's not bad to focus on the results you want, after all, this is why you're in business. You want the money, the time off, the acknowledgment, etc. However, when you focus on the activities, you're going to be more productive, fight harder, and have more fun.

So, know what you want and then focus on completing the activities that directly relate to achieving your goal.

## What Stops You

When you're stuck and can't seem to move forward or move fast enough, the usual suspect is your mind-set. If you have a fixed mind-set, it usually shows up as win/lose thoughts about your goals and progress. With the fixed mind-set, if you missed achieving your goal, then you have lost. If you hit or exceed your goal, you have won.

Using a growth mind-set, when you miss your goal ask yourself, *"How can I do better next time?"* and learn from your attempt. If you're learning, you're growing and you will move faster toward achieving what you really want.

On the other hand, if you judge the event as win/lose, this is a fixed or rigid mind-set that keeps you stuck. To free yourself, replace the unwanted thoughts and beliefs with a growth mind-set.

To begin, understand that a mind-set is a mental habit that can be changed if you want to, and it is actually quite easy to let the pattern dissolve over time when you use these five steps:

*1. Become aware of when you are using a fixed mind-set to judge your performance and that of others.*

Awareness is the first step toward change. The reasoning is that if you don't know you're doing it, you cannot change it. If you know you're doing it, then you have the opportunity to change it.

*2. Own your thoughts.*

When you catch yourself judging your or others' behavior, such as win/lose, good/bad, etc., own your thoughts and know you are being judgmental. Do not blame anyone else for them. You have them. You adopted them from somewhere or someone, so own them. They're yours now.

*3. Forgive yourself for thinking the thoughts.*

Simply say to yourself, *"I forgive myself for thinking those judgmental thoughts."* It may not feel like much in the beginning, but as you do it, the forgiveness kicks in and it gets easier to forgive yourself and others as an act of grace.

*4. Let the thoughts and any guilt feelings go.*

When you forgive, then the letting go of the guilt and judgments frees you for other growth thoughts. You also don't get to carry around the guilt forever and beat yourself up with it. I have not found any benefit in beating yourself up. In fact, letting go is much more productive and an excellent mental muscle to develop.

*5. Vow to do better next time.*

Vow to do better means that when you hear or experience your fixed mind-set or judgment, simply promise to do better at catching it earlier in the cycle. Practice the mindful catch and release, and you will get better at it. It may not feel like much in the beginning, but you'll begin to notice a distinct change in your attitude.

In the beginning, there may be a lot more unwanted thoughts than you ever thought possible. Stay with the practice. Over time, the thoughts will subside as they are replaced with the learning and growth mind-set. The process will be natural, and you'll have more mental freedom and be more effective.

# The Disrupters

Disrupters are things that interrupt your daily rhythm and flow. You may be frustrated by the fact that you can spend 10, 12, even 14 hours a day working and not achieve the results you want or only bill half of those hours.

Too often during the day, you can be taken off track by what I call Disrupters. These are things that disrupt your rhythm and flow and seem like normal activities, yet they are demons in disguise.

**The top five Disrupters:**

### 1. Your Email

How many times a day do you check your email? Some of you are constantly checking and rechecking your inbox, sometimes several times an hour. You may have a perceived expectation that you must respond immediately when you receive an email. Nothing is further from the truth. Although email is sent electronically and theoretically shows up in your inbox immediately, there is no need to respond immediately.

Focus on the work to achieve your goals as a priority. Check your email once in the morning, once after lunch, and 30 minutes before you go home.

### 2. Your Cell Phone

Mobile phones have created convenience, security, and instant access. Your cell phone may be useful during the day but steals valuable time during the evenings and on weekends when you are not at work. Learn to turn it off or at least save work calls for work hours.

### 3. Your Open-Door Policy or Not

"Hey, got a minute?" Say NO and schedule a time to chat. If you make it easy for your staff and associates to interrupt you, they will. Too often, open-door policies are set up to create clear, open communication channels. Instead, they create a clog of employees lined up at your door seeking immediate answers to non-emergent issues, and in most cases they will figure out the solution on their own.

### 4. Meetings

How many times have you been to a meeting that was scheduled to be an hour and ended up lasting three? How often do you attend unnecessary meetings or meetings that run off topic? Meetings can be a huge source of wasted time for you and others. When you're running a meeting, start on time, end on time, have an agenda, and stick to it. In a senior management or ownership position, your day may consist of back-to-back meetings, leaving only your evening hours to complete the tasks that should have been done during the day.

### 5. Habits

It's estimated that 40 percent of our daily activities are habits, not conscious decisions. Some these daily habits sabotage effectiveness and productivity.

Many people who are self-employed can't separate business hours from leisure hours. Some get caught in a time warp while surfing the Internet. Others—mainly overachievers—can become paralyzed by perfectionism or procrastination. Mainly we just don't have the tools to schedule and structure our time in a way that fits with our working style.

What you must know is that when you start to surf the web, daydream, or start doing other activities not related to achieving your goal, you probably need a short break, so take one. Get up, get out, and get refreshed.

If you take a few minutes to take a walk, you're going to come back with new energy to tackle the project. If you don't, you're probably going to still be at your desk or computer struggling for the next two hours and not make much progress.

# Rhythm and Flow

To be truly effective, you need a system that has rhythm and allows you to develop flow and momentum each day. Have you ever noticed a highly effective team in action? Professional sports teams go through a pregame routine that includes a set of exercises to get warmed up and drills to move the ball around. It's pretty much the same routine every time.

This approach establishes a rhythm that gets them in sync with each other. If you notice an individual performer before a performance, whether it's a concert or a sports event, they go through a routine to get in the flow to perform at their highest level possible.

Use the following five steps to create a positive rhythm and flow:

1. *Visualize* achieving your top three goals.

2. *Plan* your weekly appointments, activities, and tasks to support achieving your goals.

3. *Execute* your plan.

4. *Track* your activities and progress.

5. *Adjust* your activities and tasks to stay on track to achieve your goals.

# 3

# Systemize Your Business

———— 𝒯 ————

*Systems simply mean freedom.*

Whether you're a personal producer, self-employed, or a business owner, you must have systems that work to streamline the growth of your business. If you don't, your enterprise will struggle unnecessarily, you'll run the risk of being exhausted, and you won't be as effective as you could be.

Here's the good news and the bad news about systems. First, the good news: *You already have systems.* Now the bad news: *You already have systems.* I can say this with some certainty because the way you do things is your system.

Let's be honest, some of your systems work really well and others, well, not so much. Some of your systems are you doing the work. Some of your systems are others doing the work for you.

One of the biggest mistakes is to have systems that work and you're the one doing them. The other mistake is to have systems that don't work too well and you're doing them.

I'm a fan of being effective, effective being defined as *doing the* right things. Being efficient means doing things right. Have systems that are both effective and efficient is key.

There are two basic types of systems: a ***Personal Results System*** and *Business Systems*. You need both to stay on track and be effective.

## *Personal Results System*

The main purpose of your ***Personal Results System*** is to keep you on track to achieve your personal and business goals.

Your ***Personal Results System*** has three main components:

1. *Goals*
2. *One-Page Action Plan*
3. *Accountability*

*1. Goals are tools that drive action.* Clear, sharp, achievable goals that are consistent with your vision and purpose enable you to perform at your highest levels. Keeping your goals in front of you every day lets your brain automatically help you achieve what you really want.

Using this system, one of my clients remarked that goal achievement was easier now than ever before, and he's producing more.

On the other hand, I was recently working with a client's team on their goals, which I do on a regular basis. I asked the first person how she was doing on her progress to reach her goals. She said that she didn't know what her goals were! I asked her to find them, and she could not. So, she had no idea where she was in regards to reaching her goals because she didn't know what they were.

*2. A One-Page Action Plan* keeps you focused on the right activities, tasks, and projects to achieve your goals.

*One-Page Action Plan* Key Elements:

- A set of achievable steps to reach your 12-month goals

- The right activities to reach your goals

- Key "ON Your Business" projects to grow your business

- Time to renew your mind, body, and spirit

- Encouragement to give thanks and be grateful

*3. Accountability keeps you on track* by holding yourself responsible for your results. Learn what's working and what's not by tracking your progress with the 13-Week Results Dashboard or Personal Results Tracker card, so you can make adjustments on the fly to improve your productivity instead of waiting until the end of the year. Details on the **Done4You** *Personal Results System* and forms are available in the back of this book.

Using a *Personal Results System* is a paradigm shift from trying to get your way-too-long to-do list done to focusing on achieving your goals and living your vision.

# Business Systems and Outsourcing

If you're doing the accounting, writing basic sales letters, licking stamps, and filing everything, you're way too busy to be effective. You're spending your day—at your high hourly rate—on tasks that can and should be outsourced or systematized.

A good test is to ask yourself, what would happen if you took off to a hot sunny destination for three weeks and left your cell phone, laptop, and all electronic gear that ties you to your business at home? Would your business be able to continue operating?

If you said no, then this chapter is for you.

Systemizing your business is about putting policies and procedures in place to make your business operations run smoother and, more importantly, without your constant involvement. With your newfound free time, you can focus on the bigger picture to strategically grow your business.

# Why Systemize?

For most of you systems simply mean freedom from the day-to-day functioning of your organization. The company runs smoothly, makes a profit, and provides a high level of service, regardless of your involvement.

Systemizing your business is also a healthy way to plan for the future. You're not going to be working forever—what happens when you retire? How will you transition your business to new ownership or management? How will you take that vacation you've been dreaming of?

Businesses that function without their ownership are also highly valuable to investors. Systemizing your business can position it in a favorable light for purchase and merit a high price tag.

A system is any process, policy, or procedure that consistently achieves the same result, regardless of who is completing the task.

Any task that is performed in your business more than once can be systemized. Ideally, the tasks that are completed on a cyclical basis—daily, weekly, monthly, and quarterly—should be systemized so much that anyone can perform them.

Systems can take many forms, from manuals and instruction sheets to signs, banners, audio or video recordings, and outsourcing. They don't have to be elaborate or extensive, just provide enough information in step-by-step form to guide the person performing the task.

# Benefits of Business Systems

There are unlimited benefits available to you and your business through systemization. The more systems you can successfully implement and document, the more benefits you'll have. Here's a short list:

- Greater focus on long-term business growth

- Increased respect for your time

- Improved activity management

- Optimized conversion rates

- Happier customers and consistent service levels

- Increased profit and productivity

- Increased time off

- Better cost management

# Identifying Your Business Systems

The first step is to identify your existing systems. Look for the processes that have emerged as "the way we do things." For example:

Your sales process

Order processing

How the phone is answered

How the bills are the paid

How you track expenses

Some of your systems may be working effective and do not require immediate changes. Others may need some reworking. Now is a good time to check in and evaluate how well they are functioning.

# Seven Areas to Systemize

For some businesses, it may be tough to determine where to start to optimize their time and resources.

Here are seven main areas to look at. It's probably best to list all of your systems in one area at a time. Some may interact with systems in another area, and the upgrade becomes a combination shot. So, take your time and be thoughtful through the process.

Choose one system in one area and work it through. Then move to the next one. Stay with the process and evaluate how each system is affecting your business. Each business requires its own set of unique systems. The following lists are a starting point and guidelines, so feel free to create and add items as you go.

### 1. Administration

Administrative roles tend to have high turnover and therefore demand more of you and your time to train each new person. A series of documented systems reduces training time and saves you from explaining the simple things that make your business run, such as how the phones are answered when a new receptionist joins your team. Believe it or not, this takes quite a bit of your time every time you hire or outsource this service.

## Administrative Systems Checklist

| System | Have/Need | Documented | Delegated | Due |
|---|---|---|---|---|
| Opening Procedures | | | | |
| Closing Procedures | | | | |
| Phone Greetings | | | | |
| Mail Processing | | | | |
| Sending Couriers | | | | |
| Office Maintenance: | | | | |
| Watering Plants | | | | |
| Empting Trash | | | | |
| Managing Recycling Bins | | | | |
| Filing and Paper Management | | | | |
| Work Flow | | | | |
| Document Production | | | | |
| Inventory Management | | | | |

### 2. Financials

This is one area to keep a close eye on, and that doesn't mean you have to do the work yourself. Financial management systems include everything from tracking credit card purchases and invoicing clients to following up on overdue accounts. This is a prime area to outsource to an accounting firm or billing person. Get it off your desk ASAP.

These systems, as you develop them, can give you clear sets of numbers to run your business, manage your cash flow, measure growth, and help prevent employee theft. It also allows you to control purchasing and ensure that each decision is signed off and on.

## Financial Systems Checklist

| System | Have/Need | Documented | Delegated | Due |
|---|---|---|---|---|
| Commission Payments | | | | |
| Credit Card Purchase Tracking | | | | |
| Accounts Receivable | | | | |
| Accounts Payable | | | | |
| Bank Deposits | | | | |
| Cutting Checks | | | | |
| Depositing Checks | | | | |
| Invoicing | | | | |
| Tax Payments | | | | |
| Profit/Loss Statements | | | | |
| Daily Cash Out | | | | |
| Petty Cash | | | | |
| Expenses | | | | |
| Payroll | | | | |
| Purchasing | | | | |

To show you how critical proper systems are, I was working with a client to improve their sales. While interviewing one of the salespeople, I noticed a check from a client on his desk. I asked why he had it. He said that when a client sends in their payment, the receptionist opens the mail and gives the checks to the salespeople, who then give them to accounting to deposit. There was no timeline and no security process in place to safeguard the checks, and it could take days or weeks to present the checks to accounting.

I cannot begin to tell you how dangerous this procedure is, especially with the potential for losing checks, identity theft, liability, etc. I immediately met with the president of the company to explain the dire need to fix this.

### 3. Communications

Routine everyday communications such as fax cover letters, internal memos, sales letters, reports, and newsletters are a huge opportunity to standardize and systemize, to save time and ensure consistency of form and branding. They may be created from scratch by different people, but their basic headers and formats may not be much different from one another. It also takes a lot of time to train and keep training new team members.

### Communication Systems Checklist

| System | Have/Need | Documented | Delegated | Due |
|--------|-----------|------------|-----------|-----|
| Internal Memo Template | | | | |
| Fax Cover Template | | | | |
| Letterhead Template | | | | |
| Team Meeting Agenda | | | | |
| Sending Faxes Process | | | | |
| Email Format | | | | |
| Newsletter Template | | | | |
| Sales Letter Templates | | | | |
| Meeting Minutes Template | | | | |
| Report Templates | | | | |
| Internal Meetings Formats | | | | |

Scheduling _____

### 4. Customer Relations

Customer relations includes everything the customer sees or touches in your company, as well as any interaction they might have with you or your staff members.

Establishing a customer relations system will also ensure that your new team members understand how customers are handled in your business. It allows you to maintain a consistent level of high customer service, without constant training on your policies. It will also make sure that your customer relations and retention do not have to hinge on you or any other individual salesperson.

### Customer Relations Systems Checklist

| System | Have/Need | Documented | Delegated | Due |
|---|---|---|---|---|
| Incoming Phone Call Script | | | | |
| Outgoing Phone Call Script | | | | |
| Customer Service Standards | | | | |
| Customer Retention Strategy | | | | |
| Customer Communications Templates | | | | |
| Sales Process | | | | |
| Sales Scripts | | | | |
| Newsletter Templates | | | | |
| Ongoing Customer Communication Strategy | | | | |
| Customer Liaison Policy | | | | |

### 5. Administrative Assistants and Employees

Create systems in your business for hiring, training, and developing your administrative assistants and employees, if you have them. This will streamline the hiring and the time-consuming training process to develop your team into self-sufficient, capable partners.

Employees with clear expectations who work within clear structures are happier, more productive, and more motivated. Creating a clear training manual will also save you and your staff the time and hassle of training each new staff member on the fly.

### Admin Assistant and Employee Systems Checklist

| System | Have/Need | Documented | Delegated | Due |
|---|---|---|---|---|
| Systems Training | | | | |
| Recruitment | | | | |
| Incentive and Rewards Programs | | | | |
| Performance Reviews | | | | |
| Feedback Process | | | | |
| Staff Dress Codes | | | | |
| Ongoing Training and Professional Development | | | | |
| Job Descriptions and Role Profiles | | | | |

### 6. Sales & Marketing

This is an area where you probably spend a large part of your time and must be systematized to optimize your sales and marketing performance. The marketing efforts to generate new sales leads, and the follow-up to convert those leads into sales, can be systemized by creating simple systems for your basic promotional efforts.

Any one of your marketing and sales staff should be able to pick up a marketing manual and implement a successful direct mail campaign or place an effective advertisement even when you're away. Use this checklist to identify the key areas, then add or subtract from it as you and your business requires.

### Sales & Marketing Systems Checklist

| System | Have/Need | Documented | Delegated | Due |
|---|---|---|---|---|

**Sales**

Sales Process _____

Sales Order Follow-up _____

Customer Relationship Management _____

Order Processing _____

Order Delivery _____

**Marketing**

Inquiries Management _____

Referral Programs _____

Customer Retention Programs _____

Ad Creation System _____

Direct Mail System _____

Regular Promotions _____

Regular Advertisements _____

### 7. Data Management

I've often thought about how to be a paperless office. While I'm getting closer, it's not true yet. Your business needs to have clear systems for managing paper and electronic information to ensure that information is protected, easily accessed, and only kept as necessary.

Data management systems help you keep your office organized. Everyone knows where information is to be stored and how it is to be handled, which prevents big stacks of paper with no place to go.

One of the major, and underreported, reasons for a business to fail is the loss of their data due to computer equipment failure because of fire, flood, and other natural disasters. This can be prevented, especially today when we have access to the "cloud" to protect your data and systems.

Ensure that within your data management systems you include data backup systems. That way, if anything happens to your server or computer software, your data and your business are protected.

### Data Management Systems Checklist

| System | Have/Need | Documented | Delegated | Due |
|---|---|---|---|---|
| IT Manager/Management | | | | |
| Data Backup Procedures | | | | |
| Computer Repairs | | | | |
| Computer Upgrade Cycle | | | | |
| Electronic Information Storage | | | | |
| Client Files | | | | |
| Project Files | | | | |
| Point of Sale System | | | | |
| Financial Data Systems | | | | |
| Sales and Marketing Systems | | | | |
| Website Management | | | | |

# Implementing New Systems

If you've completed the exercises in this chapter, you have a good idea of the systems you currently have in place in your business. The next step is to determine what systems you need to create.

To do this, you will need to get a better understanding of the activities and tasks that you complete on a daily, weekly, and monthly basis. If you are using the *Personal Results System*, you can get a good idea of your activities and tasks by looking at the last few months.

Review your records at the end of each week and note how often you duplicate an activity or task; then group them together. From here, categorize the activities and tasks into business areas like the seven listed above, or create your own categories. If you're self-employed, pay special attention to the sales and marketing area because that's where most of your time will be spent.

Then, prioritize and plan your system creation and implementation projects. Choose one to focus on at a time based on how critical it is to your business survival and success. How long it takes to implement a system will depend on your business needs and the staff resources you have available for this process.

Remember that even the simplest system creation is a long-term process and something that will transform your business over time. Be patient, and focus on the items that hold the highest priority. You'll be surprised at how much progress you can make in just 30 to 90 days if you're persistent.

### Buy-In

It will be nearly impossible for you to develop effective systems without the involvement and input of your administrative assistant and employees. These are the people who will be using the systems and completing the tasks on a regular basis. They have the hands-on experience and details of what needs to be done and in what sequence to assist you in this process, and they can write the systems for your review and input. This will make the systemization process much faster and more efficient.

It is also important to note that when you introduce new systems, there may be a natural resistance to the change. People—including your partners, team members, and employees—are creatures of habit and can become set in the way they are used to doing things, so be patient and persistent about the projects.

**Creating Your Systems**

There are a wide variety of ways you can create systems for your business, depending on the type of system you need and the type of business you operate. Some systems will be short and simple—i.e., the format for a fax cover sheet or meeting agenda format—while others will be more complex, such as your sales scripts for a Strategy Session or sales letter templates.

One thing all of your systems have in common is steps. There is a linear process involved from start to finish. Begin by writing out each of the steps involved in completing the task, and provide as much detail as you can.

Then, review your step-by-step guide with the people who will regularly use the system, and get their feedback. Once you have incorporated their input, decide what format the system needs to be in: manual, electronic, laminated instruction sheet, sign, office memo, etc.

**Delegation and Project Management**

You don't have to do all the work yourself. The key is to delegate or outsource and follow-up with regular meetings and due dates. After all, what is the point of creating systems unless someone other than you uses them?

To make delegation work, sketch out the plans with your team members. Then give them enough freedom to complete the project within the structure of the systems that you are spending time and considerable thought creating.

## Testing Your Systems

When you create systems, you must make sure that they work. More specifically, you need to make sure that they work with and without your direct involvement.

Use both your personal and business systems for an appropriate period of time—a week or month—and notice how they work and don't work. Adjust as you go.

If you're a small business, ask for input from your staff, suppliers, vendors, and customers about how the systems are working, to see if they are seamless enough for your suppliers and whether or not they meet or exceed your customers' needs. Take that feedback and revise the system accordingly. You will rarely get the system right the first time, so be patient and persistent.

Systems will also need to be evaluated and revised on a regular basis, to ensure your business processes are kept up-to-date. Structure an annual or biannual review of systems, and stick to it.

After that, allow yourself the freedom of focusing on the tasks that you most enjoy and that most deserve your time, like creating big-picture strategies to grow your business and increase your profits—*faster*.

# 4

# Have Clients That Pay, Stay and Refer

———— $\mathcal{C}$ ————

*Do you know how much it costs to acquire a new customer?*

When it comes to marketing and generating more income, most businesses are focused outward toward getting new customers. They may have identified their target markets and created specific offers and messages for each segment. They may spend thousands of dollars on advertising and direct mail campaigns in hot pursuit of more leads, more customers, and more foot traffic.

While acquiring new customers is an effective way to build a business, it is costly, time consuming, and requires constant and consistent effort. This approach does generate results, but those results quickly disappear when the effort stops or becomes less intense.

Successful businesses that have sustained growth use a double-edged marketing strategy. They focus their efforts *outward*—on new potential customers and marketing—as well as *inward*—on existing customers and referral business.

These successful businesses leverage their marketing efforts to generate more revenue by having their existing customers buy from them over and over again.

For most businesses, this is the easiest way to increase their revenues. Simple, straightforward customer loyalty strategies and outstanding customer service are often all you need to dramatically increase your sales ... from the customers you already have.

## The Cost to Gain New Customers

Do you know how much it costs to acquire new customers?

Each new customer costs you money to acquire. You must spend your time and money on advertising, promotions, and sales expenses to generate leads and turn those leads into customers.

For example, if you have placed an ad in your local newspaper for $1,000, and the ad brings in 10 customers, you have paid $100 to acquire each customer. You would need to ensure each of those customers spent at least $200 to cover your margin and break even.

Alternately, if you spent two hours of your time and $10 per month on an email marketing program to send a newsletter to your existing database of customers, and you bring in 10 customers as a result—each customer cost you $1.

Generating more repeat business means focusing on the marketing strategies that aim to keep your existing customers instead of purchasing new ones, effectively reducing the cost of attracting new customers to your business.

These strategies are simple to implement and don't require much time investment—just a solid understanding of how to make customers want to come back and spend more of their money.

# Keeping Your Customers

Marketing strategies that focus on keeping your current customer base are easy and enjoyable to implement. They allow you to build real relationships with the people you do business with, instead of dealing with a revolving door of people on the other end of your sales process.

Repeat customers create a community of people around your business that presumably share the same needs, desires, and frustrations. The information you gain from these customers (market research) can help you strengthen your understanding of your target audience and more accurately segment it.

Remember, 80 percent of your revenue comes from 20 percent of your customers. Always focus on these customers. They are ideal customers that you want to recruit and hold on to.

# Make Them Love Buying from You

Every business—even those with excellent service standards—can improve the service they provide their customers. Customer service seems to be a dying concept in most businesses; more focus seems to be placed on the speed of the transaction. These days you can even go to the grocery store and not speak to a single sales associate, thanks to self-serve checkouts.

To improve your company's customer service standards, take a survey of your customers and employees, then use the information to create ways to have a more positive buying experience.

Customer service standards that help your customers *buy* are:

**Consistency** – The standards are kept up by every person in your organization. Expectations are clear and followed through. Customers know what to expect and choose your business because of those expectations.

**Convenience** – It is nearly effortless for the customer to spend money at your place of business. Convenience can take many forms—location, product selection, value-added services like delivery—and is also consistent.

**Customer-driven-service** – The service the customer receives is exactly how they would like to be treated when buying your product or service. It is reflective of your target market and appropriate to their lifestyle. Customers would probably not appreciate white linen tablecloths at a fast-food restaurant, but they would appreciate a 2-minutes-or-less guarantee.

### Newsletters: Keep in Touch with Your Customers

A regular newsletter is easy, effective, and inexpensive to produce and distribute. It can be written by an employee or an email marketing service subscription that can be customized to your messages and branding. The most popular type of newsletter distribution is email.

Here is an easy five-step process to starting a company newsletter:

**1. Pick your audience.** New customers? Market segment? Existing customers?

**2. Choose what you're going to say.** Company news? Feature product? New offer?

**3. Determine how you're going to say it.** Articles? Bullet points? Pictures?

**4. Decide how it's going to get to your audience.** Email? Mail? In-office?

**5. Track your results.** How many people opened it? Read it? Took action?

# Value-Added Services

Adding value to your business is an effective way of attracting customers. Every person I know would choose a mattress store that offers free delivery over one that does not. It's that simple.

There are many ways to add value to your business, including:

- **Feature your expertise.** Use your knowledge to provide additional value to your customers. Offer a free consumer guide or report with every purchase.
- **Add convenience services.** Offer a service that makes their purchase easier or more convenient. The best example of this is free shipping or delivery.
- **Package complementary services**. Packaging like items together creates an increase in perceived value. This is great for start-up kits.
- **Offer new products or services**. Feature top-of-the-line or exclusive products, available only at your business. Offer a new service or profile a new staff member with niche expertise.

Generate repeat customers in one of two ways:

**1. Impress them on their first visit.** Give your customers great service, a product that meets their needs, and then wow them with something extra they weren't expecting. Get them to associate the experience of dealing with your business with happy surprises, and create a perception of higher value.

**2. Entice them to come back.** The introduction of a new value-added service can be enough to convince a customer to buy from you again. Their initial purchase established a trust and knowledge of your business and its processes. They will want to "be included" in anything new you have to offer, especially if there is exclusivity. It is easier to attract clients who have purchased from you than potential clients who have not.

### Customer Loyalty and Incentive Programs

Another simple way to keep in touch with existing customers and keep them coming back to you is to create a customer loyalty program.

These programs do not have to be complicated or costly, and they are relatively easy to maintain once they have been implemented. These programs help you gain more information about your customers and their purchasing habits.

Here are some examples of simple loyalty programs you can implement:

**Free product or service.** Give them every 6th or 10th product or service free. Produce stamp cards with your logo and contact information on it.

**Reward dollars.** Give them a certain percentage of their purchase back in money that can only be spent on your products and services. Produce "funny money" with your logo and brand.

**Rewards points.** Give them a certain number of points for every dollar they spend. These points can be spent on your products and services, or on special items you bring in for points only.

**Membership amenities.** Give members access to VIP amenities that are not available to other customers. Produce member cards or give out member numbers.

Remember that in order for this strategy to work, you and your team have to understand and promote it. The program itself will become a product you sell.

# 5

## Attract the *Right* Customers

*"To ask the right question is already half the solution of a problem."*

– Carl Jung

When Doug, a financial advisor, first started working with me, he was struggling to set appointments with the right customers. He now has 61 appointments on his calendar over the next two months with the right potential clients.

Everyone and every business is different, so the right customer for you may not be the right client for another. I've worked with financial advisors in my "How to Find the Right Customers" courses for over 20 years, and not once have I seen the same target market, niche, sweet spot, or profile for two advisors.

The right customer for you will most often be found in your target market. Identifying your target market streamlines your sales lead generation process, because it directs you to where and who they are in the same way you find what you want at the grocery market.

# The Pareto Principle

Vilfredo Pareto was an Italian economist who noticed that 80 percent of the wealth was held by 20 percent of the population. Over time his observation has become a principle known as the 80/20 rule. It generally states that most things in life are not distributed evenly.

Used in the context of business, I've found that generally 80 percent of your revenue comes from 20 percent of your clients. The percentages can move around a bit because every business is different, but the concept holds true if you look.

# The *Right* Customers

You may say to yourself, "If I could only get in front of the right people then…"

When I work with personal producers such as financial advisors and insurance agents, their biggest issue is usually how to find more customers. They will confess that if they had more of the *right* customers, their problems would be over. They usually cover their faux pas by having too many unqualified appointments in search of the right ones.

These same people cannot answer the question, "Who is your target market?" They often assume that everyone will want to purchase their product or service with the right marketing strategy. So they waste most of their time chasing and talking with people who are probably not going to purchase anytime soon.

To streamline building, maintaining, and growing your business, you need to know your target markets that contain the *right* customers for you. Getting this wrong—or not taking the time to get it right—will cost you time, money, and potentially the success of your business.

# The Law of Attraction

The Law of Attraction basically states that your thoughts are pure energy and by focusing on what you want, you can bring more of it into your life. In order for the Law of Attraction to work, you must first know specifically what you want. If you just want more money, then just one more dollar will do because it fulfills the requirement of more money. If you want love in your life then, think this through, any love will do. An old uncle may reach out and talk to you, or an old relationship, or whatever you mean by love is going to show up.

Something else you must realize is that things do not show up all by themselves, except the weather. What you really want is going to take more energy in the form of work. I know that when I wanted to climb Pikes Peak, I worked for it; every really wealthy person who earned it themselves worked very hard for it; and athletes in every sport work extremely hard for many years to achieve their goals. Even if you win the lotto, you earned some money to buy a ticket.

I know from my personal experience that you can attract what you really want. I've wanted to be a coach for years, and now I am one; I wanted a beautiful, supportive, loving wife, and I have one; I needed a certain amount of money to pay a bill, and I got it; I have wanted a certain kind of client, and now I have them. I have seen my clients and friends attract what they really want, and they all use the same formula.

Attract what you really want formula:

1. Know specifically what you want.

2. Work and act to get it.

3. Give thanks when you receive it.

## Identifying Your Target Market

To identify your target market, begin by making a list of your customers, starting with the highest annual revenue first and working down to the least. Some of you will have just a few, and others may have hundreds or even thousands of customers. The number of clients you have doesn't matter; it's not good or bad, it's just information to work with.

Circle five of your top customers on the list and put the following information in separate columns on a spreadsheet:

- Company or name

- Business type or profession

- Geographic location

- Size

- Number of years in business

Look for similar types of businesses or professions, locations, sizes, and years in business. Note the ranges, if any. This will give you a snapshot to start with. If you have more than five companies that comprise your highest revenue list, add them in 5 to 10 at a time and continue looking for patterns. If you have more than 100 records, sort by industry and location to start to see some patterns.

You may find that you have an affinity for service businesses or the medical profession, manufacturing or distribution. This is where you can start to explore rather than talking to everyone. Target specific professions or businesses of a certain size that have been in business for the range of years that fit your profile.

If you don't have customers yet, this is going to be a bit of a SWAG (Scientific Wild Ass Guess) and serve as a starting point. Don't give up. With a little work and experimentation, you will identify a large target and then work it down to more specific facts in your niche. You may also start with your benefits, services, and products to see where they fit.

Let's go a little deeper into the profile. The next level to look at is the reasons your customers buy from you. One of the reasons is the problems you solve, and another is the solutions for those problems.

To reveal them, go through your customer list and write down under each customer's name three problems that you solved for them and the solutions provided. For example, Doug, one of my financial advisor clients, works with people who have two major problems: too much debt and not saving for retirement. The solution: a plan to reduce debt quickly while saving for retirement.

Another client, John, also a financial advisor, works with people preparing to retire. Their problem is how to retire well. The solution is a financial plan that shifts their portfolio to more income-producing investments with less risk.

Nancy, a psychotherapist client, works with people to improve their mental focus and acuity and to reduce stress caused by trauma. The solution is a course of therapy that quickly relieves their symptoms, so they can stay focused and be more peaceful while they achieve their goals.

The reasons people work with you and buy your products are because they're getting their problems solved and their needs met. Identifying the problems you solve, the needs you meet, and the benefits you provide are key pieces to discovering your target market, niche, and *sweet spot*.

As you go through this process, you may also find a gap in a market that is underserved. By creating a service or product offering for that niche, you can be extremely successful.

For example: Art Williams was an athletics coach who found a gap in the financial products and services market. He noticed that most people wanted to protect their families and save for their retirement at the same time. He promoted the concept of "buy term life insurance and invest the rest" and founded Primerica, which has grown to be one of the largest financial services companies in the world, with annual revenues of over $1 billion.

You can find underserved markets almost anywhere. For example, people wanted a reliable service to deliver flowers to their mother in another city—enter 1-800-Flowers. People wanted a handy, reliable, waterproof video camera to record on the go—along came *GoPro*. Debbie Fields baked cookies that her friends loved— others did too—and *Mrs. Fields Cookies* became a hit. You're only limited by your awareness, research, and creativity.

You don't have to be searching for the mother lode of business ideas, just ones that can be the right caliber for how you want to live and work.

## Finding the *Right* Customers

When we purchased our new red Jeep Liberty and drove it off the dealer's lot, I began to notice red Jeep Liberties everywhere.

Before then, I hadn't noticed red Jeep Liberties at all. Now they're in town, on the interstate, in parking lots—everywhere.

This is a natural process called pattern recognition, controlled by the reticulating formation at the base of your brain. Pattern recognition is what allows you to find bananas at the market, your favorite shirt, your socks, and more of your *right* customers.

The *right* customers for you have common characteristics that are a profile of what they look like and act like. This profile becomes a picture or pattern that your brain can use to find them.

In one of my all-day workshops, a financial advisor permitted me to work through his profile during the class. Along the way, he had several insights that finally clicked. When I talked with him a few days after the class, he said he'd been searching for his profile for 15 years, and on the way home he mentally reviewed every one of his clients and they all *fit* the profile. Eureka!

### The *Fit*

I talked about the *fit* earlier, and this is where it counts. The *fit* is the match between you, your services, products, your customers, and their needs and wants. The profile of the customers that are right for you reflects that matchup.

## What You Focus On Expands

When you focus on where to find the right customers, the list will expand as well the possibilities to have more of them. If you focus on the lack of customers, that will expand as well.

If you truly want to attract the right customers, execute these steps:

1. Ask yourself, "Where can I find more of the right customers?"

2. Appreciate the customers you have that are right for you.

3. Research where to meet and how to connect with the right customer.

4. When you talk with people, talk with them as if they are your best customer.

5. Every time you meet someone new, give thanks for getting closer to the right opportunity.

## Being in Position to Win

Great sports coaches often speak about being in position to win. Sports is a good analogy, because it's easy to see the principles at work and the results are final—they win or lose. In your case, being in position means going to the right places to meet the right people with a proven reliable process to win.

## A Proven Process

Let me be direct: It does you no good to go to the right place with the right people without the right skills to win! Having a *Proven Process* to win is critical to your ongoing success.

Let me take you through the process I use and teach my clients to attract the right customers.

### The *Less Than 30-Second Commercial*

By now, you've heard of and probably tried to use the 30-second commercial or elevator pitch. It doesn't matter what you call it: The purpose of using it is to pique interest in you and what you do for potential clients to start a conversation.

Unfortunately, some of you wind up saying way too much and for way too long to be effective or interesting. Let me show you the rules of how to use the *Less Than 30-Second Commercial* opportunity to your best advantage.

*Rule 1. Be yourself.*

*Rule 2. Be yourself.*

*Rule 3. Keep it short.* People have a short attention span, so you must grab their attention quickly.

*Rule 4. Provoke a conversation.* The overall goal of your brief encounter is to pique interest in talking with you further.

*Rule 5. Use this Less Than 30-Second Commercial format:*

1. Your name

2. Your title

3. Your company

4. Your product or service

5. One big benefit

6. *SHUT UP and wait*

*Rule 6. Go for the next step when they're interested.*

Remember, you're not trying to get them to buy your product or service during these first steps. Your mission is to *connect*, provoke a conversation to pique their interest, and set up the next touch step such as a coffee meeting. That's it.

### The Coffee Meeting

This meeting can be an in-person sit-down affair with coffee or a phone conversation. The purpose is to *connect and qualify* them for the next step. The formats for the meeting and the phone call are pretty much the same; you're just using different modes to communicate.

When you're calling or meeting in person, start by reintroducing yourself and where you met, then ask how much time they have to talk today. Say that you want to get to know them and their business. Have a few questions prepared to get the party started.

As the conversation develops, you can talk about anything that interests you and them. It could be food, family, fun, hobbies, or business. Listen, if you find something that you connect with them on, go with it. That's at least half the objective of the meeting.

Using this format, I've had conversations with people about all sorts of things, some of which I knew little about before we began talking. I was genuinely interested in them, so they didn't mind my naïve questions about their interests and were flattered that I had even asked.

Enjoy the process and remember: If you cannot connect, the odds of making a sale go down to almost zero. When you connect, the odds of making a friend and a sale go up.

### Coffee Questions

My coffee meetings follow a natural flow and format. I'm naturally a curious person and really want to get to know people. I let the conversation develop as it would when I'm talking with a friend.

The questions I use are designed to *connect with and qualify* a potential client, referral partner, and connector. The basic flow is to ask general questions about them, how they got into their business, and the problems they're having.

When they ask about my business, I give my quick *Less Than 30-Second Commercial* and wait for them to ask more questions. As we talk, I ask questions that reveal if the problems they're having are ones that my coaching and accountability service can solve.

When they're interested in learning more about working with me, I invite them to have a private Strategy Session to identify what's stopping them and how to fix it, and to have an up-front conversation about how to work together. When they say yes, we set an appointment. If they're not interested or not a fit, I arrange to stay in touch.

With this approach, I win no matter which way the conversation goes and I'm often surprised at what happens. I've met new friends, new referral partners, I've had people sign up for my courses, coaching, and MasterMind Groups, or I just meet someone new.

### Strategy Sessions

The purpose of the Strategy Session is to uncover the client's pain in full detail so we can create a plan to fix it together. Once the appointment is set, I email the Strategy Session Pre-Work to the client. It usually takes about 30 minutes to complete the form.

The Pre-Work form has three main sections:

1. Client information

2. Business problems

3. Desired coaching outcomes

During the sessions, I lay out the Pre-Work in front of me and go through each question in detail so the client can see what I'm doing, what I'm seeing, and why I'm seeing it. I hold nothing back, and I'm completely transparent during the process.

The promise I make is that during the session, you'll learn what stops you and basically how to fix it, and we'll have a direct conversation about the best way to work together.

About 80 percent of the people I have a coffee meeting with agree to a Strategy Session. Ninety percent of the people who complete the Strategy Session agree to participate in a program with me.

## Connectors and Clients

During most business meetings, you'll have the opportunity to meet new people either at your table, in the food line, or at a networking session. This is an excellent opportunity to expand your network of connectors, clients, and partners.

A *connector* is someone who is in a position to introduce you to more clients, partners, and other connectors. So, if you're a financial planner, you may want to be introduced to someone who will refer clients to you, such as an accountant or a property and casualty insurance agent. If you're a property and casualty insurance agent, you probably want to be introduced to a real estate agent and mortgage broker.

While you're at the event, you're also looking to connect with the *right potential clients*. Again, when you meet new people, you want to connect with them to start the sales process, not sell them your service or product at the event.

I met a commercial real estate broker at a networking breakfast. We exchanged cards and agreed to have a coffee meeting. Charlie and I met at a local coffeehouse in the afternoon. We spent an hour and a half talking about everything but business. We both had other appointments, and as we were leaving, Charlie said, "Oh, I have an interest in coaching!" I said, "I'll call you tomorrow," which I did, and he became a client. My main focus was on *connecting*—not selling my service—and I used my coffee questions with him on the phone.

# Networking or Not

How do you learn to network? What I've most often seen at networking events is that everyone is watching everyone else to learn how to do it—and no one really knows. So, everyone winds up working with bad habits and techniques that don't work.

When that happens, you spend two or three hours talking with your friends, then you leave tired and disappointed again.

We spent several months researching networking events to discover what really works. I'll spare you the details of what doesn't work.

Here's what works:

1.  Be yourself.
2.  Connect with five new connectors or clients at every event.
3.  Agree to have a coffee meeting to get to know them.
4.  Don't quit until you have met your goal every time.
5.  Call them to have or set up a coffee meeting.
6.  Use your coffee meeting format to determine the next step.

Here's why this works. Have you ever met someone at an event, and they have agreed to call you? How many times have they actually called? I've met over 2,000 people in the first few years of building my coaching practice, and I can count on the fingers of one hand the number that have called me. Yet, when I've called, at least 90 percent of them have agreed to meet.

Most of you go to networking events and meet no one new, let alone a new potential client, connector, or referral partner. Instead, you spend the time chatting with friends and colleagues. If you sincerely want to improve your sales, try this: Meet five new contacts and go home.

I have met five new people in one hour and gone home. My work was done for that event. I call them the next day as promised and use my coffee questions to start the sales process. It's usually a fun conversation, and they're appreciative because no one else calls. We have the opportunity to get to know each other, and from there I get new clients and connectors in a fraction of the time it used to take.

## Attracting the *Right* Customers

If you can find bananas in the grocery market, you can find and attract the *right* customers. It's all about knowing what you're looking for, being in position to win, and having a proven process you can rely on to build your business—*faster*.

# 6

# *7 Simple Sales Steps*

---- *c* ----

*Sales is a process not alchemy.*

The ability to sell effectively is a skill set that everyone who is self-employed must develop and master. It's one you'll continually practice and improve throughout your career, to be and stay as successful as you want to be.

Contrary to popular belief, you don't have to be the most outgoing, enthusiastic person to be successful at sales. You don't even have to be a good public speaker. All you need is to:

- Sincerely care about your customers as people.

- Listen to their problems and needs.

- Have genuine passion for what you're selling.

- Use a basic sales process.

Originally I developed the *7 Simple Sales Steps* as a way to diagnose problems clients were having with their sales performance so we could fix them one step at a time. As I worked clients through their issues, the steps developed into an effective, straightforward sales process that can be used by almost everyone in sales.

# The *7 Simple Sales Steps*

One of the first things to understand is that sales is a process that can be broken down into clear steps to streamline and increase the odds of making a sale.

The sales process varies according to the type of business, type of customers, and type of product or service that is offered; however, the core steps are the same. Similarly, sales training varies from individual to individual, but the core skills and steps remain the same.

The *7 Simple Sales Steps* are a framework that can be adapted to suit your unique products, services, industry, business, profession, and personality. Remember that each step is critical because it builds on the previous step. It's essential to become adept at each step, instead of solely focusing on closing the sale.

### Step 1: Lead

A *Lead* is defined as someone who has *declared an interest* in your product or service. They have either responded to a marketing campaign or told you that they are interested.

*Your first priority is to connect with them.* Connecting is the primary way to build a relationship and is the foundation upon which to build the sale. It's an ongoing process that matures over time and experience with each other.

*Connecting* is the beginning of the sales process and increases the odds of making a sale. If you don't connect, then your odds of making a sale go down to almost zero.

The best tip I can give you about connecting and making a positive first impression is to first be interested in them and their business. If you're sincerely interested in them, then usually they become interested in you. To make this point, imagine you're having coffee with someone and all they do is talk about themselves. How interesting is that?

Compare that to meeting with someone who's truly interested in getting to know you. What do they do? Usually, they're asking natural questions about you and what you've done, how you came to do it, what made you think of it, and so on. For example, suppose you mentioned that you took a trip to Napa, California. The next natural question might be, "What interests you about Napa?" You would then go on to explain your interest in making wine and how it's been an interest for several years, the wine tasting, hot mud baths and a massage, or whatever.

The point is you're having a real conversation. You begin to connect in a deeper way. This is what I mean by *connecting!*

How did that happen? It happened because you're genuinely interested in them and they're genuinely interested in you.

Let me ask you, "Have you ever been with someone who is just making a small talk conversation so they can get to the sale?" You felt it, right? How did it feel? To me it feels shallow and manipulative, and I just don't trust them, let alone want to buy from them. Here's the point: If you and I can feel it, so do others.

Being genuinely interested in other people is the keystone to *connecting*. It's being in the moment and asking *the next natural question* to find out more. Master this and you'll master *connecting*.

### Step 2: Qualify

*Qualifying is a two-way street.* You're working to find out if the customer is match for your product and services, and they're working to figure out if you can be trusted and solve their problems.

The three objectives are to:

1. *Connect* and build trust.

2. Discover if there is a *fit* with their needs and your products and services.

3. Determine the *Next Step* in the process.

*Connecting* and trust are the foundation to discover the *fit* between the customer's problems, needs and wants, and your products and services. The *fit* is critical, because if the client doesn't have problems that your product or service can solve, then there is no need to go any further in the sales process.

As you get to know your client, use open-ended questions to *connect* and discover the problems that keep them up at night. If you're a professional advisor, such as a financial advisor, consultant, accountant, or coach, a powerful approach is to have a Strategy Session with the client. The Strategy Session is a scripted private meeting with the client to discover and go deeper into their problems and how they affect their life and business, and to have a frank conversation about the best way to work together.

When I say "scripted" here, I mean a series of questions that you can ask the client to discover their problems and ways to solve them. Use a combination of open-ended and closed-ended questions to learn their needs, problems, and motivation to solve their issues such as:

- What is your biggest problem about (something your product or service fixes)?

- How long has it been a problem?

- Ask clarifying questions about their responses, to fully understand how big a problem it is.

- Ask how they want to fix it, with a question like, "Is this something that you want to fix?"

As you go through the process, if there is a *fit*—which means that you and the client agree that the client does have problems you can solve—and they want to fix it, then you can move to the next step. If there is no *fit* and no desire to solve the problem, there is probably no potential for a sale. It's that simple.

If you continue to push for a sale, this is where you become a *pushy* salesperson, and this is probably not what you really want.

At this point, if there is not a *fit,* then you can politely agree not to continue the sales process with them; ask for a referral to someone who might benefit from your service or product.

Listen closely: 'It's OK NOT to get the sale if there is NOT a *fit* or if the customer just does NOT want what you have to offer. BE SMART AND MOVE ON.

### Step 3: Present

*It's ShowTime!* You have now determined that your potential client needs your service or product and they're interested to see how it can work for them.

Your major objective in this step is to *build the value* of your solution by *connecting* with the client through the problems you have discussed and then *present* your solution by showing how you can solve their problems with your product and/or service.

This step requires skillful handling to present the problems and build agreement that, in fact, these are the critical issues that must be solved now. The cleanest way to build value and agreement is to present the problems that have been agreed to as critical issues, and discuss how your solution can solve them and the value they will bring to the customer.

Note: Don't ever, Ever, EVER present your solution until the client has been qualified and has expressed interest. If you present too early, you are in danger of becoming a pushy salesperson and ruining your chance of a potential sale. It's difficult to recover from this position.

### Step 4: Commit

As you *present,* this is the time when you build agreement with the client that your services can solve their problems and you ask the client to *commit* to your solution. There are three possible answers:

1. Yes!

2. No.

3. Tell me more.

Obviously, yes is the preferred answer.

If the answer is no, then you must uncover why they do not want to move forward. It could be a budget issue, a timing concern, or something else. The objective at this point is to discover how and when they would want to proceed. Usually, a combination of open-ended and closed-ended questions can be used to sort out what's going on. This is where your skill and perception as an astute salesperson come into play.

There are many variations of this situation, and the best advice I have is to prepare for the ones that most often come up so you're ready to handle them confidently and assertively.

Here's a classic format to help clients work through issues:

- Repeat the issue back to the customer to ensure that you understand them correctly and that they know you understand them.

- Empathize with what they have said, and then provide a response that handles their concerns.

80

- Confirm that the answer you have provided has resolved their issue by repeating it to the customer.

When the answer is "tell me more," the process is straightforward. Ask them what they need to know, then shut up and let them talk. Often they will talk themselves right into the sale, if you let them.

The emphasis here is on finding out more about the situation and to help the client talk through how to solve the problem. The more you try to solve it, the worse it usually gets.

### Step 5: Deliver

OK, the client said yes! Here's what to do.

1. Deliver on time.

2. Deliver as promised.

Forget about the "under promise and over deliver" concept. If you just do what you say you're going to do, that is usually enough to provide exceptional service. Here's why. Has someone ever told you that they would call you on a certain day and then not called? Has a company promised to deliver your new washer on a certain day and time and not shown up without calling?

Compare that to when someone says they will call you at 9 a.m. on Tuesday and they do it! Or when your new washer is delivered during the time window that was promised. Or the repairman shows up on time.

These events seem miraculous because they were simply done when promised. When that happens, how do you feel? Usually, pretty good, and you're happy with the company too.

So, keep your word. And if you do break it, clean it up. The odds are that you'll WOW your client as you build their trust.

### *Step 6: Follow Up*

This is the time to distinguish yourself and your company once again. You may be afraid to call the customer after the sale is completed, because they may cancel or perhaps they're unhappy with something.

This is exactly the time you must *follow up,* and here's the secret sauce:

1. Call them and ask, "How are you doing?" If they're upset, they will usually tell you right then. When they're thrilled, ask for permission to use them as a testimonial or reference.

2. If they didn't tell you about any problems, *Be Brave* and say, "The product or service was delivered last week. How is it doing or performing?" Or ask, "How do you feel about it?" They will tell you. If they got scared or have buyer's remorse, this is the time to reinforce the reasons they purchased.

3. If something isn't working, find out what it is and arrange to fix it immediately. Stay in touch throughout the process. When it's resolved, you get to *Be Zorro!*

These calls will serve to *connect* and build trust, to help ensure that they become a loyal, repeat customer and that they will refer new clients to your business.

When I was selling at Hewlett-Packard, one of my biggest and best customers ordered new server racks. At this time, HP and Compaq had just merged. The customer had some older racks, and the new ones did not connect with the older models.

I sent the recommended parts to fix the problem. Once the parts arrived, the customer called and told me that the parts I sent didn't work and that they had to have them to complete their project on time. This was not what I wanted to hear. I took full responsibility to figure out a solution and promised to call the manager every day to report my progress.

It seemed that no one in HP at the time was sure of a fix. I found a savvy server rack product manager, and together with his team, we sorted out the rack connect ability issue. As we worked the problem, I continued to make my daily calls to the manager. I usually got his voice mail. I left a message every time to update him on my progress. When the new parts arrived, they worked. The customer went on to purchase more servers, desktops, and other computer equipment from me as they upgraded their systems and purchased other companies. It feels really good to be Zorro.

### Step 7: Referrals

Referrals and introductions are natural extensions of the relationship you have built with your new client.

There are three main benefits of asking for introductions and referrals:

1. *Access* to the client's suppliers, complementary businesses, colleagues, and organizations, instead of having to make cold calls.

2. *Leverage* the trust and credibility you have built.

3. *Leads* to new sales opportunities.

It's amazing how many of you don't ask for referrals or have a weak way of asking. If you're not asking, what may have happened is that you have stopped trying because you have run out of ways to ask and actually get a referral.

What I've found is that 10 to 20 percent of your clients will never give you an introduction or referral, and 10 to 20 percent will spontaneously give them to you. So that means 60 to 80 percent of your clients will give you an introduction or referral if you ask.

An introduction simply means that you're requesting to be introduced to someone or to a company. Most clients will do that for you. It doesn't mean it's a sale. It means you're going to have the opportunity to meet someone in your target market, niche, or *sweet spot* to see if they are ready to talk with you about how you can help them. When you explain how you've helped your client, the new introduction has the opportunity to declare their interest.

If they're not ready yet, ask them if it's OK to stay in touch and if it's OK to put them in your customer database to keep in touch on a regular basis with newsletters and an occasional phone call. Usually they will agree, and you have permission to build your relationship with them.

With the new client, be sure to *follow up* with a handwritten thank-you note and consider including a gift card to their favorite coffee shop as well. From time to time, give them a phone call or drop by to ask how they are enjoying the product or service, and if they have any further questions or needs you can assist them with. This contact opportunity will also allow you to ask for a referral or even an up sell. At the very least, it will nurture your relationship with the client.

## Improve Your Sales

The *7 Simple Sales Steps* are an effective strategy to dramatically improve your sales process and your sales. When I'm working with clients who are struggling with their sales, what I usually see is that they skip steps.

As an example: If the client is meeting a lot of people and not closing sales, the issue is usually that they are skipping the *Qualify* step and going from "Hi" to "Do you want to buy?" If the client is making sales and not getting more *Leads,* the issue may be during the *Referrals* step.

Skipping steps is like omitting key ingredients when you're baking a cake. A basic cake recipe includes flour, milk, butter, salt, vanilla, and a leavening agent such as baking soda. If you omit the baking soda, the cake won't rise and you'll have a flat cake. If that's what you want, then that's OK. If it isn't, then … well, you get the picture.

The overall concept of the *7 Simple Sales Steps* is to *Sell Step-to-Step,* which means that all you have to do on each step is to sell the very next step. So, when you meet someone, all you need to do is sell them on having a coffee meeting with you to get to know each other.

At the coffee meeting, you're working to see if they have a need for your service or product by asking a few simple questions. If they have needs or problems you can solve, they become a *Lead.* When they're a *Lead* and interested in going further, then set up a Strategy Session to *Qualify* them. When they *Qualify,* go to the *Present* step, and so on. It's really that simple.

The *Sell Step-to-Step* graphic on the next page is the same one I use in my classes to illustrate the process. Follow the steps from left to right. Sometimes you may have to review a stage to prepare the customer to move forward.

*Connecting* is the overarching piece to building a relationship as the foundation of the sales process. *Referrals* can become a *Lead* to start the process again.

If the client is not qualified—no need, no interest, no pain you can fix—then politely close the meeting and move on. They will appreciate it and you'll have more time to attract a new lead.

*Sell Step-to-Step*

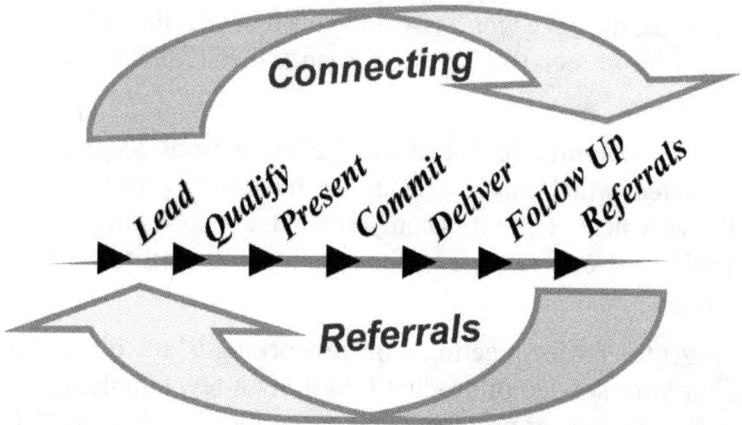

Connecting

Lead  Qualify  Present  Commit  Deliver  Follow Up  Referrals

Referrals

When Doug, a financial advisor, first saw the system, he thought that it would slow down his sales and business building. After using it for over a year, he finally told me that it actually sped up the process. Over 90 percent of the people who complete a Strategy Session with Doug choose to work with him, and his annual income has tripled!

# 7

# Generate High-Quality Leads

———— $\mathcal{C}$ ————

*"Fast is nice, but accuracy is everything."*

– Wyatt Earp

When I ask some of my clients where their *best* customers come from, I usually get an answer that is equivalent to "I don't know." When we look at the source of their *best* clients, we discover they came from their target market.

Clients who have lead generation issues usually don't have a reliable, systematic way to continuously identify new potential customers. Their efforts and processes are usually too cumbersome and inconsistent to produce the quantity and quality of leads required to grow their business. They wind up spending up to 80 percent of their time scrambling for leads.

There is hope! Build a system.

The first step toward having more high-quality leads is to discover their source and quality. Once you know what they look like and where they are, you can find more of them.

# Generate High-Quality Leads

Begin by listing all the sources of your leads for the last three months. Then write the number of leads and number of new customers next to the source using the format below.

| Source | # Leads | # New Customers |
|---|---|---|
| Referral | | |
| Networking | | |
| Word of Mouth | | |
| Direct Mail | | |
| Internet | | |
| Advertising | | |
| I Don't Know | | |
| Other | | |

*Circle the three sources with the most leads.*

Next, calculate your lead-to-customer conversion rate. Simply divide the number of new customers by the number of leads and multiply by 100.

**# of new customers ÷ # of leads x 100 = percent conversion rate**

For example: 3 new customers from 10 leads looks like this:

**3 new customers ÷ 10 leads x 100 = 30 percent conversion rate**

Calculate the conversion rate for your top three lead sources:

| Source | # Leads | # Customers | Conversion Rate |
|---|---|---|---|
| 1. | | | |
| 2. | | | |
| 3. | | | |

# Quantity or Quality of Leads

You may now begin to see that based on conversion rates, the number of leads may not be as important as the number of new customers from a given source.

So what affects leads turning into customers? Are you in the right target market? Do you need to improve your scripts? Adjust your product or service? Find a competitive edge?

Maybe. But the first step toward improving your conversion rate is to evaluate the leads you're currently generating.

### What Is Quality Lead?

A common assumption is that a lead is a lead. Anyone who calls in for a quote or who you meet should be convinced to purchase from you, right? Not necessarily true!

In the case of a property and casualty insurance agent, anyone can call in for an auto insurance quote. Most of the time, they're just shopping for the lowest rate with no hassles. I've found that these types of leads do not make good long-term clients for the insurance agent.

They will usually switch companies the next time the rate increases, or they'll shop for the lowest rate again in six months. Plus, they usually don't buy any additional insurance products. The net is that the agent actually loses money on these clients.

A high-quality lead is someone who is looking to purchase and values your service and products. These customers are the best *fit* and are the leads to focus on generating.

### Attracting High-Quality Leads

Generating high-quality leads on a consistent basis requires a system that must include the following components:

**1. Goals.** Always know the results you want from a given activity or program. Set goals using the Item X by Time Y formula to structure the program.

**2. Purpose.** Always know the intent of your program. Design your message and delivery method, and offer to achieve those results.

**3. Target market.** Focus on attracting the right customers in your target market. Know their age, sex, income, and purchase motivations from their profile. From that information, you can determine how best to reach the right customers.

**4. Powerful offers.** People love to buy and hate to be sold. Craft offers that are timely and irresistible. Offer additional value-added services that have a high perceived value and low cost to you. The primary purpose of the offer is to entice them to talk with you; without that, you really don't have a lead.

**5. Consistency.** Even a blind squirrel can find a nut. Attracting high-quality leads is an ongoing process to establish timing in the marketplace. Your mailing or phone call may not be at the right time for the customer. Sometimes you'll get a good response with your first attempt and then stop. This kills the momentum of your campaign. The key is to have consistent delivery of your message on a schedule you can manage and afford.

**6. Tracking.** Knowing how a campaign is performing is critical to its survival and your success. Establish a workable way to track the performance of each campaign every day, week, and month; then adjust as required to achieve the project's goals. Many times, a campaign has been stopped yet it's working beautifully. If it's working, keep doing it.

**7. Follow-up.** Once a lead is generated, make sure you have the resources and determination to follow up on them. Be diligent, aggressive, and timely. Sometimes the customer is not ready to purchase the first time you meet or talk with them. Over time, things change and you should be in position to win.

Here's the danger in not following up. As a service provider—a financial planner, insurance agent, carpet cleaner, telecom services provider, etc.—this scenario happens too often. You've done all the work, and the client says, "No, not at this time." You're disappointed, of course, pick up your proposal, and leave. Time goes by. Things change in their life and business. Your potential customer now sees the value of your proposal and wants to move forward immediately, but can't find your card.

The next day, that customer meet another person who is qualified and eager to help, and he gets a windfall sale. You did all the work, and the next guy through the door gets the business. Don't let this happen. Develop a follow-up system and stick to it.

# Connecting

Lead generation at its core is connecting with your market. You usually don't have to implement an expensive array of new marketing strategies. With a little tweaking and refinement, you can easily attract more high-quality leads using an existing program. Of course, if you don't have a program, you'll need to create one.

Use the following strategies to immediately improve the results of your existing programs or to use with a new one:

*1. Court Them.* This may sound strange, but marketing is a lot like dating: You must woo the customer. First, send a letter of introduction that educates and makes an enticing get-to-know-you offer of a free service.

Follow with additional letters, newsletters, and offers that continue to educate and explain how critical it is that they buy from you and no one else right now.

Sometimes people will throw your letters away two or three times before they're ready and motivated to act. Schedule the letters or email ahead of time and stick to it. People want to know that you're reliable and trustworthy. Continuous contact reinforces those feelings.

Imagine that a coupon arrives in the mail with a buy-one-get-one-free offer from a new local restaurant. Two weeks later, you have the time and are in the mood to try something new, but where is that restaurant offer? The next day, another coupon from the same restaurant shows up in the mail with the same offer. "Wow! How lucky can I be?" you exclaim.

Is this a sign from the universe or a strategic play by the restaurant?

This is an example of how a repetitive campaign works. The frequency can be weekly, every two weeks, monthly, every two months, etc. Experiment a bit to find out what works. It's a huge mistake to just send one mailing and expect a huge return.

*2. Craft Special Limited Offers.* Create an offer that's too good for the right customers to refuse. Describe how you cater to their unique needs, wants, and problems.

A financial advisor targeting families could offer a free college savings plan to open a door. Or target people ready to retire by offering free retirement income analysis. The young married and the mid-career executive offers would be different as well. The point is that each offer will be different from one target market to another.

*3. Grab Them.* When making an offer, use a compelling headline to grab attention. Newspapers and magazines use this every day to drive sales. State the biggest customer benefits, or feature an unbelievable offer such as "How to Double Your Retirement Savings."

*4. Spark Curiosity.* Don't give all the information needed to make a decision to buy. Instead offer a Free Special Report that will answer all their questions. In this report, go into detail about how big the problem really is, how it can be fixed, and how to contact you for a complementary appointment. Using this approach, one chiropractor had almost more business than he could handle.

# Leverage

Time is your most valuable asset. Use systems to leverage your time into results. The following systems help you be more effective and profitable:

*1. Referrals.* People love to help other people—it's a basic human need. Give customers an opportunity to help their friends, colleagues, business partners, vendors, and suppliers.

This is one of the most cost effective, profitable, and beneficial ways to attract the right customers. And the beauty is that once your referral system is set up, it often runs itself.

Referral systems are also an excellent way to leverage your existing client base. Reward them with discounts, gifts, or free service in exchange for a successful referral. You'll be surprised at how much goodwill is generated by 5, $10, or $20 coffee gift card.

When new customers are attracted by coupons for free services or products, offer the same free product or service to their friends. Do the same with their friends. This ongoing program will bring more business than you can imagine.

My number one strategy to connect with new high-quality leads is to simply ask to be introduced to a specific person or type of person. Simply say that you would like to meet Joe Smith at the XYZ Company and ask if that person knows him.

Often they do and will introduce you.

The PersonalResultsAcademy.com has several types of proactive referral systems that can be implemented for almost no cost except for your time.

*2. Strategic Alliances.* Forge marketing alliances with businesses that provide complementary and noncompetitive services and products to the same target market. Create cross-promotion and cross-referral direct mail campaigns that mutually benefit the alliance's businesses.

For example: A carpet cleaning and water damage services company can co-market with a house cleaning service, a plumber, a roofer, and a heating and cooling company. None of these businesses compete for the same service or product, and each of their customers can use the other company's services.

The alliance can advertise and send direct mail to their geographic target markets with all the businesses represented on one postcard or ad. The possibilities are endless. The advertising and direct mail costs will be a fraction of what it would cost if each company executed its own campaign.

*3. Advertise.* Statistics show that nearly 50 percent of all purchase decisions are motivated by advertising. Create direct response ads that motivate customers to contact the business for more information using curiosity, mystery, and urgency with an almost unbelievable offer.

As always, target the right audience with ads placed prominently in publications that your audience reads. This doesn't mean to fork over the cash for expensive display ads. Inexpensive advertising in email newsletters with cooperating alliance partners is effective and carries the trust and creditability of your partner.

*4. Direct Mail.* The secret to improving your results is to craft direct response offers specifically for the right customers in your target market. It's one of the fastest and most effective ways to reach out to potential clients and leads you're developing into customers.

Try sending thank-you notes to customers and leads that you have just met, to foster the relationship and build trust.

## Lead Management

As you develop a lead generation strategy, put together and use a system to manage, track, and follow up on the leads. Without such systems, the leads you have paid for are prone to being mismanaged, which results in missed opportunities for new customers and sales.

Gather information on leads to suit your business based on your target market profile and what can be realistically asked for from potential customers. Basic profile information includes:

- Contact name
- Title
- Company name
- Mailing address
- Phone number
- Cell phone
- Email address
- Website address
- Product and service of interest
- Problems and needs

- Time frame
- Source of lead
- Competitors of interest
- Alternate contact person

The simplest way to gather and manage your sales lead data and history is with an electronic database program specifically designed for Customer Relationship Management (CRM), but you can also use a hard copy system to get started. Here are a few proven ideas:

**Electronic Database Programs**
- High level of organization
- Data-entry required
- Unlimited space for notes and history
- CRM such as SalesForce.com and Infusionsoft
- Software programs such as MS Outlook, MS Excel, and MaximizerCRM
- Business card scanners such as CardScan or Neat

**Index Cards**
- Variety of sizes: 3x5, 4x6, or 5x8
- Contact information on one side
- Notes on the other side
- Easy to organize and sort

**Rolodex System**
- Easily organized and compact
- Contact information on one side
- Notes on the other side
- Keeps phone conversations and purchase details

**Notebook**
- Use for small lists
- Managed by one person
- Room for lots of notes

- Inexpensive
- Difficult to reorganize

**Business Card Organizer**
- Use for lists of under 100 contacts
- Limited space for notes
- No data entry required
- Rolodex-style or clear binder pages

When business cards are in small piles all over your desk, it's almost impossible to find a specific card quickly. As soon as it's found, it's placed in another stack. Also challenging is how to determine which pile to search: Is it by first name, business name, product, by must-call-today, or ...?

For example, when you want to call Harry and the cards are organized by company, finding Harry is going to take awhile, especially if there are several stacks of cards. Then, after you have called him, his card is going to be placed in a different stack, which will take another 30 minutes to find when you want to call him again.

When my assistant first suggested a business card scanner, I was hesitant because it was another piece of computer equipment I had to buy and learn to use. But it made sense. I bought one, and it totally changed my mind.

I now sort through my electronic stack of cards to find Harry in a few seconds, not 15 to 30 minutes, and I don't have piles of cards all over my desk. Plus, I can sort through the cards by company, first name, last name, type, etc.

Systems are leverage in your business that multiply your effectiveness, profitability, and sustainability. You don't have to execute all the strategies or systems to be effective. Pick the one that provides the greatest return of your time and money investment, then find a way to make it work.

Once you know what you're looking for, then you can find more of it. Don't quit. Once a system is in place and working, you may consider adding another as long as you maintain the existing system.

When I work with financial advisors and service providers, we work diligently to develop their referral strategy and system. Once we work it through, it almost runs itself, and their business builds—*faster*.

# 8

# Create Powerful Offers

*Make them an offer they can't refuse.*

Irresistible offers make your customers think, "I'd be crazy not to take him up on that" or "An offer like this doesn't come around often." They instill a sense of emotion, desire, and urgency to act.

Your irresistible offers can be used to:

- Build your email list
- Generate leads
- Increase sales
- Convert leads into customers
- Drive traffic to your website or business
- Move old product

## What Makes a Powerful Offer?

A powerful offer is one that makes the right customers respond and take action. It gets people running to spend money on your product or service.

Powerful offers nearly always have an element of urgency and of scarcity. They give your audience a reason to act immediately, instead of putting it off until a later date.

Urgency relates to time. The offer is only available until a certain date, during a certain period of the day, or if you act within a few hours of seeing the ad. The customer needs to act now to take advantage of the offer.

Scarcity refers to quantity. There are a limited number of spaces, products, or supplies available for the offer. Again, this requires the customer to act immediately to reap the high value for low cost.

**Powerful offers also:**

- **Offer great value.** Customers perceive the offer as having more value than a single product on its own or than the product at its regular price. It is clear that the offer takes the reader's needs and wants into consideration.

- **Make sense to the reader.** They are simple and easy to understand if read quickly. Avoid percentages: Use "half off" or "2 for 1," instead of "50 percent off." There are no catches or requirements, no fine print.

- **Seem logical.** The offer doesn't come out of thin air. There is a logical reason behind it, such as a holiday, end-of-season, or anniversary celebration, or a new product. People get suspicious of offers that seem "too good to be true" and have no apparent purpose.

- **Provide a premium.** The offer provides something extra to the customer, like a free gift or free product or service. They feel they are getting something extra for no additional cost. Premiums are perceived to have more value than discounts.

Remember that when your target market reads your offer, they will be asking the following questions:

1. What are you offering me?

2. What's in it for me?

3. What makes me sure I can believe you?

4. How much do I have to pay for it?

# The Most Powerful Types of Offers

Decide what kind of offer will most effectively achieve your objectives. Are you trying to generate leads, convert customers, build a database, move old product off the shelves, or increase sales?

Consider what type of offer will be of most value to your best customers and will make them act quickly.

### Free Offer

This type of offer asks customers to act immediately in exchange for something free. This is a good strategy to use to build a customer database or mailing list. Offer a free consultation, free consumer report, or other item of low cost to you but of high perceived value.

You can also advertise the value of the item you are offering for free. For example, "Act now and you'll receive a free consultation, worth $75." This will dramatically increase your lead generation, and allow you to focus on conversion when the customer comes through the door or picks up the phone.

### The Value-Added Offer

Add additional services or products that cost you very little, and combine them with other items to increase their attractiveness.

This increases the perception of value in the customer's mind, which will justify increasing the price of a product or service without incurring extra hard costs to your business.

### Package Offer

Package your products or services together in a logical way to increase the perceived value as a whole. Discount the value of the package by a small margin, and position it as a "start-up kit" or "special package." By packaging goods of mixed values, you will be able to close more high-value sales. For example: a free yoga class when you buy a package of six Thai massages.

### Premium Offer

Offer a bonus product or service with the purchase of another. This strategy will serve your bottom line much better than discounting. This includes 2-for-1 offers, offers that include free gifts, and added services for purchases over a specific dollar amount.

### Urgency Offer

As I mentioned above, offers that include an element of urgency enjoy a better response rate, as there is a reason for your customers to act immediately. Give the offer a deadline, or limit the number of spots available.

### Guarantee Offer

Offer to take the risk of making a purchase away from your customers. Guarantee the performance or results of your product or service, and offer to give the customer their money back if they are not satisfied. This will help overcome any fear or reservations about your product, and make it more likely for your leads to become customers.

# The Crux of Your Marketing Campaign

A powerful offer is more often than not the reason a customer will respond. It is how you generate and then convert leads into loyal customers. The more compelling and valuable the offer is, the better the response will be.

Many companies spend thousands of dollars on impressive marketing campaigns in glossy magazines and big city newspapers. They send massive direct mail campaigns on a regular basis, yet don't receive an impressive or massive response rate.

These companies do not understand that simply providing information on their company and the benefits of their product is not enough to get customers to act. There is no reason to pick up the phone or visit with you right now.

# Create Your Powerful Offer

### 1. Pick a single product or service.

Focus on only one product or service, or one product or service type, at a time. This will keep your offer clear, simple, and easy to understand. This can be an area of your business you wish to grow or old product that you need to move off the shelves.

### 2. Decide what you want your customers to do.

What are you looking to achieve from your offer? If it is to generate more leads, then you'll need your customer to contact you. If it is to quickly sell old product, you'll need your customer to come in and buy it. Do you want them to visit your website? Sign up for your newsletter? How long do they have to act? Be clear about your call to action, and state it clearly in your offer.

### 3. Dream up the biggest, best offer.

First, think of the biggest and best things you could offer your customers, regardless of cost and ability. Don't limit yourself to a single type of offer; combine several types of offers to increase value. Offer a premium, plus a guarantee, with a package offer. Then take a look at what you've created, and make the necessary changes so it is realistic.

### 4. Run the numbers.

Make sure the offer will leave you with some profit—or at least allow you to break even. You don't want to publish an outrageous offer that will generate a tremendous number of leads and leave you broke. Every customer has an acquisition cost, as well as a lifetime value. The amount of their first purchase may allow you to break even, but the amount of their subsequent purchases can make you a lovely profit.

## Powerful, irresistible offers attract the right business to you.

# 9

# Profit over the Phone

———— $\mathcal{C}$ ————

*Reach out to connect with someone.*

For some, the word *telemarketing* brings to mind annoying telephone calls you get at dinnertime or in the middle of your favorite TV show. For others, it may conjure up images of rows of people with headsets, working from far, far away.

You may think it's an old-fashioned marketing strategy. In some cases this may be true, but telemarketing is still an important tool for every business, of every size, to use effectively.

In fact, telemarketing is reemerging as a powerful way to generate leads, close sales, and conduct research. Done well, it's an efficient and cost-effective strategy to build your business.

What if I told you that you're already using telemarketing as a regular part of your business? Every time you pick up the phone, you're engaging in a telemarketing process. Every time someone on your team picks up the phone, they too are engaging in a telemarketing process.

Telemarketing is not just a system for cold calls. It's organized communication between you and your clients using the phone. So, telemarketing is one-on-one phone work on a larger scale to connect with your customers, prospective clients, and target market.

Let's talk about how to turn the phone work/telemarketing you're already doing into a profitable marketing strategy for your business.

# Telemarketing for Your Business

A common misconception is that telemarketing needs to happen on a broad scale in order to be effective—that pages and pages of potential customers must be cold-called on a daily basis and that businesses must hire dozens of staff members to conduct and manage the efforts.

As mentioned above, telemarketing is any communication with your potential or existing clients over the phone. Regardless of the size of your business, the telephone can be used effectively to generate more leads and convert more sales.

The key benefits of establishing an organized telemarketing system are:

- Instant access to identify and reach key decision makers.

- One-on-one interaction that can develop real relationships with empathy and trust.

- Minimize cost and spend less on sales outreach and research.

**Who Are the Best Telemarketers?**

Success with telemarketing has a lot to do with the personality of the caller. Generally, the best telemarketers have the following qualities and abilities:

- Warm and friendly
- Positive attitude
- Good phone manners
- Strong listening skills
- Empathy
- Energy and enthusiasm
- Belief in your company and its products
- Ability to think on the spot
- Good organizational skills
- Ability to handle rejection
- Skillful at qualifying potential customers

# The Telemarketing Process

There are two types of telemarketing: outgoing and incoming. You should have a proactive strategy in place to handle both types.

Remember that your approach to telemarketing must have a clear purpose and objective to be effective. What is the purpose of the call (outgoing and incoming)? Is it to inform? Set up an appointment? Establish a need or desire? This will help guide how you handle each type.

What are the objectives, and how will you measure the success of your program? Number of appointments? Number of new customers? Number of referrals? Sales volume?

### Incoming Calls

When a customer calls your business for the first time, you should have a system in place to make a great customer service-oriented impression. Some of these customers will have seen one of your advertisements, received a direct mail piece, or be responding to other elements of your marketing campaign.

Your telemarketing system for incoming phone calls can take the form of:

- An answering service
- Voice mail
- A messaging service
- An order-taking system
- An information providing system

The person or people who answer the incoming calls should be well trained for the role and clearly understand the expectations for handling them. Your receptionist should be trained thoroughly in the products and services you sell in order to answer basic customer questions intelligently. Your team should know how to answer the phone according to your company policy and have excellent phone manners.

Consider including the following instructions in your incoming telemarketing system or process:

- Answer the phone after two rings and before four rings.

- Have a standard company greeting. Include your company name, as well as the name of the person answering the phone.

- Record sufficient information from each caller to ensure proper follow-up: name, phone number, reason for call, the action required, and who is responsible for it.

- Get back to someone placed on hold in 30 seconds or so. When you're on hold, it seems like an eternity even though it's only been 10 seconds. You may want to take their name and number and have their call returned promptly.

- Give a short description of your company and what makes you different from your competitors during the phone call.

- Always repeat back any information or agreement exchanged.

- Be the last one to hang up.

## Outgoing Calls

Outgoing calls are the more challenging aspect of your telemarketing strategy. In this case, you are proactively asking your customer for something, as opposed to responding once they've already been convinced to act.

You can use an outgoing telemarketing strategy to:

- Set appointments

- Generate leads

- Make cold calls

- Update databases

- Follow up on direct mail and other campaigns

- Convert leads to sales

- Conduct research surveys

Outgoing phone calls engage the person on the other end to begin building a relationship based solely on verbal communication and without the assistance of the many nonverbal cues and physical behaviors. Depending on the type of call, you will be seeking to:

- Connect

- Attract their attention

- Spark their interest, needs, or desires

- Motivate them to act
- Seek agreement

It is essential to the success of your outgoing telemarketing efforts that you create a script for each type of outgoing call your company makes. This will keep you and your staff focused on the purpose of the call and give you tools and prompts to keep you on track. We will review scripts for telemarketing later in this chapter.

Here are some simple steps for making your outgoing telemarketing efforts a success:

### Know who you are calling

Do your research. Know exactly who it is you need to contact at each company. Is it the manager or vice president? Owner or CEO? Once you know who you are targeting, you can do some research prior to your phone call, and ensure you call at a time that is convenient. You will want to know a bit about their industry as well as the company and their role within it. If you have served another client in the same industry, let them know.

When you have them on the phone, confirm that the basic information you have is correct (name, title, etc.). If you do not know who the best person to speak to is, ask the receptionist for the name of the person who makes purchasing decisions related to your product.

### Be prepared; stay organized

Have all the materials you may need in front of you, and clear your desk of any distractions. Be prepared to record key elements of the conversation for action or later discussion. Also, keep a record of all the calls you make and the results of each call. This will prevent you from making duplicate calls, which do not reflect well on your organization, and help you track messages you left, as well as the most productive times of the day for outgoing phone calls.

### Know why you are calling

As I mentioned above, your phone calls should be purpose-focused. Are you calling to set up a meeting? Introduce yourself and your products? Get them to try what you have to offer? Keep this clear in your mind and stick to it.

### How to Reach a Decision Maker

Reaching a busy decision maker can be a challenge. You may talk with them on the first try, or it may take several attempts. Be patient and have a plan of attack.

First, identify the right person to talk to. Often you may be pursuing someone you think is the decision maker and find out much later that it's actually someone else. You can use the person who answers the phone as your personal concierge to help you. It may be the receptionist, administrative assistant, secretary, or even another executive who can help if you're charming enough.

One of the greatest needs we all have as human beings is to help others. Often the receptionist spends time endlessly answering the phone and transferring calls all over the company. They do get weary of it and may not feel appreciated. They will usually jump at the chance to help you if you ask. These are powerful allies to develop, and they can help you get the job done faster.

Personalize your relationship with each person you talk with. They're people, not things, so treat them as you would treat a friend. They are gold. They know the company because they work there and really know who to talk to about what. So, it's smart to use them as a guide.

Here are some guidelines for developing a relationship with your personal concierge.

- Take the time to connect with them.

- Tell them your name and company.

- Tell them why you are calling.

- Ask their name and write it down.

- Get an understanding of their position and responsibilities.

- Stay positive and confident.

- Never pitch the receptionist on your product.

- As you develop your relationship, ask them to help you pin down the decision maker by asking, "What's the best way to talk with (name)?" Often they will tell you the best time to call.

Once I was calling a vice president of sales for a medium-sized company. Each time I called, I talked with his admin assistant, and she would tell me he was in a meeting or out of the office or… . After the third call, I said nicely, "Sue, I've called several times for Bob, and I can't seem to reach him." She said, "Yes, I know. What can I do? He's really busy. I start at 8 a.m. He comes in at 7 and answers his phone." I said, "Thank you" and hung up. Guess what I did the next day at 7 a.m.? Yep! And I had a detailed conversation with him.

### Be persistent

Persistence pays off, especially when it comes to large potential accounts. You may have to call many times before you can work your way to the right person. Expect this and stay positive, and your persistence will pay off.

### Develop strong phone skills

You can create a great first impression on the phone when you cultivate excellent phone communication skills. Pay attention to the tone of your voice, whether or not you are smiling, the pacing of your sentences—slower is better—and general phone manners. Ensure you clearly identify who you are and what company you work for every time you speak to someone new. Although you may have a lot to do, be sure to be warm and friendly. This pays off big-time in developing the real relationship you want.

# Telemarketing Scripts

Scripts are essential to successful telemarketing. You'll benefit by having a "plan of action" for every type of phone call that your company makes. This will also ensure that each staff member has a consistent approach, which is part of your branding.

We discussed the importance of scripts and writing scripts earlier, and I encourage you to review this section before you craft your telemarketing scripts.

### Script Components

#### Greeting: Opening the Conversation

**Incoming calls** should be handled with a consistent, friendly greeting that informs the customer of what company (or department) they've reached and who they're talking to.

**Outgoing calls** need to engage the customer quickly, just as a headline needs to catch the reader's attention instantly. Say just enough to pique their interest and have them listen, then say why you're calling. The four basic steps are:

1. Hi, (Their Name), I'm (Your Name).

2. I'm with (Your Company).

3. The reason I'm calling is ... (Be straightforward.)

4. Do you have a minute to talk? (If they don't, arrange a time to call back.)

This format is a simple, straightforward way to open a conversation. I've made thousands of personal and client calls, and this is the one that consistently works. It allows the person you're calling to quickly know who you are and what you want, and is the beginning of developing a relationship.

To understand this process, look at your own needs when you get a call. You want to know right away who is calling and why. If you don't get that critical information, you usually become suspicious and guarded, which are the two killers of outbound calls. You must begin to build trust immediately.

**The Reason for Your Call**

If you don't tell them why you're calling, they won't listen to anything until you do. So tell them directly the reason for your call, and ask if they have time to talk.

When they're ready, ask permission to outline the call. This shows that you have given the phone call substantial thought, organized your information, and respect their time.

**Asking Questions**

Information gathering is an essential part of both incoming and outgoing phone work. Ask questions to develop the conversation, and encourage your customer to fully express their problem, circumstances, and concerns. Sometimes their questions may not relate specifically to what the call is about. That's OK because as you listen and explain, you're building a relationship with the customer, which can yield valuable firsthand information that can be added to your market research.

For incoming calls, your first priority is to connect with the customer. Listen to their question(s), then request permission to ask them some questions to clarify the issues before you answer theirs. Having a real conversation builds relationship and allows you to solve their problems in a spirit of cooperation and trust that builds your brand experience.

### Two Types of Questions

**Open-ended questions** cannot be answered in one word. They encourage the customer to provide explanations that give insight into their needs and opinions.

**Closed-end questions** can be answered with one word, usually yes or no. They provide information quickly and succinctly. They are good for gaining commitment, but may not be the best way to get your customer talking.

### Qualify the Opportunity

When you're making a sales call, be sure to prepare and ask questions about the following key topics to be sure you're talking to the right person and that they're in a position to make a decision.

- **Responsibility:** Who is in charge of making the decision? Is it the same person who will be making the purchase?
- **Budget:** How much financial resources are available for your product/service? What is the budget? What influences this number?
- **Time frame:** When does the customer need the product or service? When will the transaction and delivery process have to be completed by? What is the reason for these deadlines?
- **Competition:** Who else is the customer talking to? What will impact their decision? What aspects are they comparing?

### Obtaining Agreement

You and the customer must agree on what their problems and issues are before a sale or a resolution can be made. To help with this process at key points throughout the conversation, you need to know you're on the same page as your customer. An easy way to do this is to simply ask them an open-ended question such as, "How are you feeling about what we've been discussing so far?" or "OK, let me recap where we are right now. You have problems A, B, and C. They're causing X, Y, and Z for you. Correct?"

Once you have agreed to their needs and problems, then move on to how they can use your service or product to solve their problems. Finding out that they agree with you and your solutions is a powerful method of persuasion that builds relationships, leads directly to a satisfactory resolution, and sets up the sale.

### Overcoming Objections or Not

Objections seem to be the nemesis of some salespeople. The problem is when objections are seen as obstacles instead of opportunities to educate the client.

If the customer is hesitating to purchase, there may be hidden questions that must be answered before they can move forward.

The smart play is to brainstorm all potential reasons, doubts, and issues you can think of that will come up during a call. Then develop empathic responses to each one.

A simple chart that looks like this is a helpful tool to refer to during your call:

| Customer Issue | Response |
|---|---|
|  |  |
|  |  |

Remember to respect the client's issues as they are raised, and treat each point the customer makes as a legitimate one. Show empathy and relate to what they have to say. Phrases like "I can see how that would be a concern for you," "I used to think the same thing," and "Sure, that's completely understandable" allow you to relate to them, establish common ground, and then share how other customers overcame their doubts.

If the client continues to hesitate to purchase, you may want to ask them about some of the doubts and concerns on your list to uncover the hidden objection. The worst thing to happen is that you'll know what the client is thinking and feeling, and then be able to work them through the issues.

If the client is not ready to commit to a purchase, find out the next step.

**Closing with Commitment**

Once you have opened the conversation, developed a relationship, asked questions, secured agreement, and resolved issues, all you have to do is close the conversation by asking for a commitment.

The commitment should be your objective for calling or a step toward that objective. For example, if the purpose of your call was to set up a meeting, ensure that you commit to a time and place before you end the conversation. If your objective is to make a sale, you may need to make a few phone calls or hold a few appointments to achieve that.

Assume that if you have gotten this far, you have the sale. Be confident, and use phrases like "How about we meet on this day at this time?" and "Where can I send the product?"

You will want to confirm whatever you have committed to in writing with your customer. If you have set an appointment, send them a quick note to thank them for the phone call, and put the meeting in writing. Remember to be as polite and succinct as possible. Avoid lengthy emails and letters.

# Tips for Effective Telemarketing

Communicating with your existing and potential customers over the phone requires a different set of skills than in-person communication. Make sure you choose the best people for this job. When you only have your voice to communicate, you must be aware of the impression you're giving to the person on the line.

### Smile

This may seem like a silly point to put at the top of this list, but it is important. Your caller will be able to hear if you are smiling and will interpret your smile as enthusiasm. You will sound more positive, friendly, and open to dialogue. Remember, the person on the other end can hear everything, so avoid multitasking (drinking water, eating, and unnecessary typing) while you're on the phone. The guideline is, if you can hear it, so can they.

### Be a good listener

Once you get your customer talking, listen. They will be giving you important insight into their purchase motivations and their potential objections. Take notes as you listen, and never assume you know what they are going to say. After long periods of speech, check in and repeat back what you have heard, to confirm you heard it properly. Make sure to leave a pause between what they have just said and what you are about to say. This shows that you have been listening and are not jumping in at your first opportunity.

## Call at an optimal time

Knowing who you are calling will ensure that you contact them at the most appropriate time—the time they are most likely to answer your phone call. For example, business owners will need to be reached during business hours. Try to reach them during quiet times—usually first thing in the morning or just before the close of business. If you are calling consumers, then make your calls in the evening when they are most likely to be home.

## Use a familiar tone

You only have your voice to establish a new relationship with a potential customer. The tone you choose is just as important and has just as much impact as the words you choose. Use a tone that is friendly and confident, and resembles the way you would speak to your friends.

## Be prepared to handle rejection

No matter how targeted your contact list, how amazing your script, or how great your approach, rejection is an inevitable part of outgoing telemarketing. Learn to quickly let go of a "no" as a rejection and move on. Some people will not only reject what you have to say, they'll be rude in doing so. Remember not to take this personally. They could be having a bad day or just not have enough time to listen to what you have to say. Consider asking to call back at a better time, or just shrug it off. The longer you hang on to it, the worse it can get.

## Be prepared to handle difficult customers

Difficult customers will appear on the other end of the phone line for both incoming and outgoing calls. This is another inevitability of telemarketing and of business in general. Again, remember not to take what they have to say personally. They just want to air their frustrations and be heard. Listen intently, stay calm, and try to empathize with what they have to say. Use calming language, never interrupt, and record as much as possible about what they are saying. Then, promise to follow up—allowing yourself to take time to consider how you would like to handle the problem— to try to resolve their issue quickly.

### Make the call standing up

When you are standing, you will sound more confident, authoritative, and decisive. Your diaphragm is expanded when you are standing, which will increase the confidence in your voice. Do this for the important phone calls—the big accounts.

### Have strong phone manners

Here are some tips for ensuring you have a strong, professional phone presence:

- Ask for the contact by name, not role or title.

- Use your full name when you're asked who is calling.

- Clearly state your company name.

- Tell them why you are calling.

- If you do not reach your customer, ask for the best time to reach them.

- Do not hold. Call back instead. Your time is valuable, too!

When I'm calling my personal style is to talk with you as if you're a friend, to *connect*, have a conversation and, of course, be true to the purpose of the call. Use a script to guide the flow instead of controlling it to improve your results.

# 10

## Use Scripts to Increase Sales Immediately

— *C* —

*What do playbooks, prompts, guides, and scripts all have in common?*

*They are useful tools to keep you on track to achieve your goals.*

Playbooks are used by coaches to show sports teams how to overcome an opponent. Prompts help kick-start writers and other creative professionals when they're stuck. Guides provide directions so you can complete or implement a specific task.

Film scripts tell actors how to act their role. In business, scripts are tools that guide you through customer interactions and conversations with more predictable results. They're a way of maintaining the consistency of sales presentations, training, and skill building. There may be a single script or several, and the scripts may change regularly or be the same for years.

Here's the good news and the bad news about scripts. You already have and are using them. They are just not written down.

Here's proof: If you record what you say in certain circumstances, you'll find that you're saying the same things almost every time the same way. That's your script. Some examples are: your 30-second commercial, your sales presentation, and how you answer your phone. They're scripts.

## Do You Really Need a Script?

The short answer is yes! You absolutely need a script for your customer interactions. They improve your effectiveness by maintaining the conversation's intent and flow for consistent positive results.

If you're self-employed, the chances are you're already a pretty good salesperson. If you have not identified your scripts, then you could only be working at half of your true potential—or half of your potential earnings.

Scripts don't have to be "cheesy" or read verbatim. They act as a map for your sales process and provide prompts to trigger your memory and keep you on track. How many times have you made a cold call that didn't work out the way you wanted it to? Scripts can dramatically improve the effectiveness and efficiency of your sales processes.

Your sales script is a living, breathing, changing member of your sales process and deserves just as much time and effort as your marketing collateral. Memorize and rehearsed them like a film script, then use your personality to breathe life into the conversation, while staying focused on the call's objectives.

## Are Your Scripts Working?

If you're currently using written scripts in your business, how are they working? Are they as effective as they can possibly be? How do you know?

Scripts are like any other element of your marketing campaign: They need to be tested, measured, and then changed based on what is or is not working.

Measure the success of each script based on its purpose and desired results. For example, if the purpose of your script is to convert leads into sales, track the number of sales that are being converted from the leads.

When evaluating your existing scripts, ask yourself the following questions:

1. **How old is this script, and what was it written for?** Scripts are members of your company. They need to be written and rewritten and rewritten again as the needs of your customers change, your product or services change, and as new strategies are implemented.

2. **Does this script address all the customer objections you regularly hear?** Every time you hear a customer raise an objection that is not included on the script, add it. The power of your script lies in the ability to anticipate customer concerns and answer them before they're raised.

3. **Does this script sound the same as the others?** Your scripts are part of the package that represents you, your company, and your brand. There should be a consistent feel and approach throughout your scripts and presentations so that your customers will recognize and feel confident.

4. **Is everyone using the script?** Who regularly uses these scripts? Just the junior staff? Only the top-performing staff? Make sure everyone is singing from the same song sheet. Your customers will appreciate the consistency.

# Types of Scripts

Depending on the product or service you offer and your marketing strategy, there are countless types of scripts you could prepare for your business.

When you sit down to create your scripts, start by making a list of the circumstances when you interact with your existing or potential customers. Then, prioritize the list from most to least important, and start writing from the top.

**Here are some commonly used scripts and their purposes:**

### Sales Presentations

Each time you make a presentation, use the same or a slightly modified version of your script. Each client and each circumstance is different. However, the basic flow of each presentation will be the same. This script starts with a confirmation of the reason for the meeting; moves on to the discovery of the problems and pains the customer wants to cure, the benefits and features of the product or service, and a list of possible objections with responses; and ends with a closing sequence.

### Closing the Sale

Use a list of questions and statements as prompts to set up and close the transaction. The script includes a list of possible reasons why a customer may want to wait to purchase, with planned responses to promote the sale.

### Incoming Phone Calls

Everyone who calls your business should be treated the same way. If you're representing a company, start with the company name and then your name. If it's your direct line or mobile phone, answer with your first name. When you're working for a large company, they may have standards that you must follow.

### Cold-Calling

This is one of the most important scripts to master for your business. You must quickly grab a busy person's attention, then connect and qualify them for the next step. As a starting point, use your *Less Than 30-Second Commercial* to start the conversation to navigate to the right person to talk with.

### Direct Mail Follow-Up

Scripts for outgoing calls that are intended to follow up on a direct mail piece are essential for every direct mail campaign. They are designed to call qualified leads that have already received information and an offer, and convert them into customers. These scripts should focus on enticing customers to act and on overcoming any objections that may have prevented them from acting sooner.

### Market Research

Scripts used primarily for market research focus on gathering information. Use a combination of open-ended and closed-ended questions to build relationship and encourage honest dialogue.

### Difficult Customers

Just like you need to practice the sales process, you also need to practice how to handle difficult customers. A proper script will help you diffuse the situation by calming down and resolving the customer problem.

### Objections or Not

Objections are simply questions that have not been resolved yet. Part of your job as a salesperson is to uncover the client's questions early, so you can handle them during the sales process and not near the end at crunch time.

## Creating Scripts

Creating powerful scripts is not as complicated as you may think, but it will take some time to complete. Focus on the most vital scripts for your business first. State the purpose of each and how the results will be measured, so you can sort out what's working and what's not.

## Your Script Binder

Keep master copies of all of your scripts in one organized place. An effective way to do this is to create a binder, and use tabs to separate each type of script. The binder can be a physical hard copy, electronic files, or both.

Create separate tabs for all the customer concerns, doubts, worries, issues, and problems you have ever heard in relation to your product or service. Group them by categories so you can find them easily.

Then, list your responses next to each one, with several responses to each concern, doubt, worry, issue, and problem for each type of customer. A master list of customer issues and responses is an invaluable tool for anyone who is self-employed, a salesperson, or script writer. The more responses you can think of, the better.

Remember, the script binder is never finished. You will need to make sure that it is updated and added to on a regular basis.

# Writing Scripts—Step by Step

### Step 1: Record What You're Doing

If you aren't using scripts—or even if you are—start by recording yourself in action. Record yourself on the phone and during in-person customer interactions. Make notes on your word choices and body language. You may also wish to ask an associate to make notes on your performance and discuss them with you in a constructive fashion.

Also note the customer's reactions and body language, in responses to qualifying questions, and closing statements.

### Step 2: Evaluate How and What You're Doing

Look at your notes, and ask the following questions:

- How are you engaging the customer?
- Are you connecting and building trust?
- Are you uncovering their needs and problems?
- What qualifying issues are you avoiding?
- Does your presentation make sense to the customer?
- What problems or issues are raised?
- Is your offer a powerful one?
- Are you being polite and respectful?
- Is your closing sequence natural and reveal the next step?
- Are you being effective?

Once you have answered and made notes in response to these questions, make a list of things you need to improve and how you think you might go about doing so. Do you need to strengthen your closing statements? Do you need to brainstorm more responses to objections? Remember that everyone's script and sales process can be improved.

Take it one step at a time, and improve each day.

### Step 3: Decide Who the Script Is For

The first part of writing a script—or any piece of marketing material—is having a strong understanding of who you are writing it for. Who is your target audience? What does the right customer look and act like?

Review your target market and customer profile characteristics such as age, sex, location, income, occupation, and marital status. Be as specific as possible. What are their purchase patterns? What motivates them to spend money?

### Step 4: Decide What You Want to Say

There are typically five sections of every script—and there may be more, depending on the type and purpose of the script.

*A. Connect*

- Establish common ground.
- Ask if this is a good time to talk.
- Be yourself and build trust.
- Get their attention and pique their interest.

*B. Qualify*

- Find out if this is the right person to be talking with.
- Guide the conversation by asking questions from your script, to understand their needs and motivations.
- Use open-ended questions that cannot be answered with a "yes" or "no."

### C. Present and Develop Agreement

- Develop agreement on how your service or product can help them.
- Repeat the key points back to the customer to gain agreement.
- Ask questions they will respond to with "yes."

### D. Handle Customer Concerns and Questions

- Anticipate issues based on customer comments.
- Repeat the customer's concerns back to them so they know you have heard them.
- Use your own and other customers' experiences to show how others had the same issues and worked through them.
- Ask about any remaining concerns or doubts as you close.

### E. Closing for the Next Step

- Be confident and natural.
- Ask, "Have I answered all your questions?"
- Ask, "What would you like to do next?"
- Then ask a transactional questions, such as a start date, delivery timing, and payment method.

**Step 5: Make It Your Own**

The most important thing about a script is its intent and flow. You must make the script your own for it to work effectively. Adjust the scripts to suit your own style while maintaining the intent, flow, and overall objectives. Be clear what elements of the script are company standards, required elements, and essential techniques.

I use a written script when I'm working with clients on their referral presentation. First, I say it to them so they can hear that it works and that it sounds natural. Then I have them say it back to me so they become comfortable with it. Often on the third or fourth attempt, they will confess that the script doesn't feel authentic, it sounds phony. So, I take the paper back and have them say it their way. When they do, it sounds natural, contains the proper elements, flows, and it works.

If you're writing a cold-call script, write a presentation that is strong on connecting with and qualifying the customer. Use words that your target audience will understand, relate to, and resonate with.

Use sensory language that can trigger emotional and feeling responses: "You'll need this," "This will solve your problem," "You'll feel better when you have this," etc.

### Step 6: Continually Revise

After you have carefully crafted your script, put it to the test. Practice on your colleagues, friends, and family. Get their feedback, and make changes. Be sure it sounds natural, builds relationship, and achieves the call's intent.

As your scripts evolve and new products or services are introduced, add the new scripts to your script binder.

Track the results you're getting and adjust your presentation to be consistent with your goals. You may also wish to record and evaluate your performance on a regular basis as a tool for skill development.

## Script Tips

1. Sales is a conversation, so make the script yours. It should look, feel, and sound like you naturally do, not like you're reading off the page—unless you have some required information that must be read verbatim per government laws or statues.

2. Practice anticipating and eliciting real issues, concerns, and doubts—including the ones your customer doesn't want to raise.

3. Continually think of responses to customers' issues and how to handle them. Each issue could have several responses, geared toward specific customer types and doubts.

4. Anecdotes are persuasive writing tools—use them in your scripts. People enjoy hearing stories, especially stories that relate to them and their experiences, frustrations, and troubles. Let the story sell your product or service for you.

5. Spend time on your closing progression. This is a critical component of your presentation and phone call, and can be the most challenging and fun part of the sales process, once you have mastered it.

6. Include body language reminders in your scripts—they're just as important as your words.

7. Create ease and trust by mirroring and matching your client's posture, arm position, seating positions, and voice pace.

8. Change your body posture to see if they change as well. If they change to match yours, you're in sync. If not, ask a few questions to re-sync and get on track.

9. Spend time with the masters. If there is a salesperson you admire, ask to observe them in action. Take notes on their performance and the techniques they use for success.

10. Confidence sells. Notice your fears and self-talk. Then focus on connecting with your client to overcome your fear of failure.

11. If your script is not successful, ask the customer why not. Even if you don't get the sale, you'll get a new situation you can craft responses to and never get stumped by it again.

12. Failure is part of the learning process and is an opportunity to grow and improve your skills.

13. Practice, practice, practice.

Telemarketing is one-on-one phone work to connect with your target market, niche, potential customers, and clients. Use this opportunity to build trust, educate, and sell to build your business—*faster*.

# The Next Step

———— $\mathcal{C}$ ————

*Vision with action can change the world.*

You've learned 10 Strategies to Build Your Business–*Faster!* To begin to make your dreams real now's the time to "put a stake in the ground" for what you really want.

The next step is to create a realistic 12-Month *Action Plan* with a set of achievable steps to reach your goals.

The three KEY elements of an *Action Plan* are:

1. Clarity: clear, sharp goals to fulfill your vision
2. Focus: doing the *RIGHT* activities to achieve your goals
3. Accountability: accepting responsibility for your actions

Putting together an achievable 12-Month *Action Plan* with clear sharp steps and accountability is absolutely the most critical piece of the achievement puzzle and increases your odds of success.

Take a few minutes to dream, plan and act.

Stay focused. Enjoy the ride.

## *Connect* with Jack

I'd love to hear how you're using these strategies and the results you're getting in twenty-five words or less.

Please email me at JackRand@JackRand.com

If you would like to set up a speaking engagement for Jack, please send an email to:

info@JackRand.com

Sign Up for the Quote of the Week and Jack's latest tips and insights. JackRand.com

# *Programs*

Transform your productivity, effectiveness and results.

### *Personal Results System*™

Plan, execute and hold yourself accountable to be more effective, improve your productivity and have more fun.

### Personal Vision Course

This is a unique opportunity, like a mini-retreat, to think through what you really want, set goals, and put together an action plan to streamline your success with a proven system that works.

### Attract the *Right* Customers Course

Discover the clients you love to work with that are hiding in plain sight.

### MasterMind Groups

Work with other self-motivated business people to achieve more together than you could alone.

## Private Coaching

One-on-one sessions designed to breakthrough self-imposed barriers.

### PersonalResultsAcademy.com

E-Learning available 24/7 to build your business – *faster!*

For More Information Go To: www.JackRand.com

# *About the Author*

Jack Rand Coach, Speaker, Author

For over 30 years, Jack has worked with self-employed service professionals and executives to improve their sales performance. He's known for his ability to guide, focus, build confidence, and in a friendly conversational way he inspires you to take action.

His *Results Focused Coaching*™ is a straightforward, outcome-orientated approach to discover what you really, really, want; focus on the *right* activities, renew your energy and enjoy your success.

While at Hewlett-Packard he was Tops in Sales, MVP, and a Sales Excellence Coach.

Jack has a Bachelor of Arts Degree in Speech Communications.

His hands-on, interactive workshops transform your ability to have what you really want.